A Beautifully Solemn Scene

THE LEWISBURG CEMETERY

PENNSYLVANIA

Robert M. Dunkerly

HERITAGE BOOKS
2013

HERITAGE BOOKS
AN IMPRINT OF HERITAGE BOOKS, INC.

Books, CDs, and more—Worldwide

For our listing of thousands of titles see our website
at
www.HeritageBooks.com

Published 2013 by
HERITAGE BOOKS, INC.
Publishing Division
100 Railroad Ave. #104
Westminster, Maryland 21157

Copyright © 2013 Robert M. Dunkerly

All rights reserved. No part of this book may be reproduced or transmitted in any form or by any means, electronic or mechanical, including photocopying, recording or by any information storage and retrieval system without written permission from the author, except for the inclusion of brief quotations in a review.

International Standard Book Numbers
Paperbound: 978-0-7884-5472-1
Clothbound: 978-0-7884-6902-2

Table of Contents

Foreword v

Lewisburg: Port on the Susquehanna 1

The Rise of Rural Cemeteries 3

The Town Needs a Cemetery 6

Cemetery Tour 41

Notable Burials 57

Other Prominent Burials 75

Facts & Figures 95

The Cemetery Today 97

Sources 98

Foreword

Lewisburg, Pennsylvania is a wonderful place to appreciate history. The town has fortunately preserved its sense of place, with a vibrant downtown and excellent examples of historical architecture.

The Lewisburg cemetery and its burials reveal connections with the town's collective past. Like all cemeteries, it reflects the community's history and culture, especially that period when the cemetery was created. The cemetery is therefore a gauge by which to measure the impact of events, both local and national, on a small town. The cemetery also includes many prominent citizens: early founders, local leaders, and celebrities. Three congressmen, four professional baseball players, a president of Bucknell University, one Medal of Honor winner, and over 600 military veterans from each of the nation's conflicts through Vietnam rest here.

As Union County commemorates its 200th Anniversary in 2013, it is appropriate to not only reflect on the region's past, but on the historic sites that serve as tangible links to the past. Along with well known and well loved local sites like Packwood House, Slifer House, the Civil War monument, and the county courthouse, this author contends that the Lewisburg Cemetery is an under-appreciated treasure.

Perhaps the cemetery is not as well known as it should be, yet it deserves a rightful place alongside the other historic sites of the town. It is hoped that the cemetery will be recognized by residents and visitors alike for its importance to the town's history, and for its architectural beauty. May it continue to inspire and be a place of reflection, as it has been for over one hundred and fifty years.

This work has been immensely satisfying, and has reinforced my admiration for Lewisburg's history and architecture. In compiling this book, I used many resources and tried to be as accurate and up to date as possible. I hope readers will forgive any oversights. I appreciate feedback, and will make corrections in a future edition.

RM Dunkerly, Richmond, VA. October, 2012

Acknowledgements

Many people assisted with this project. I would like to thank Holly O'Brian, Elaine Wintjen, and Carol Manbeck with the Union County Historical Society, Andrew Miller of the Susquehanna Valley Convention and Visitors Bureau, Cemetery Association members Diane Meixel, Nancy Neuman, and Brian Bickhart, and Lewisburg residents- and former teachers- Joe Keller and Bernie Blamble, Lee Troup with Christ Lutheran Church, Sharon Dittmar of First Presbyterian Church, and Tena Keister with the Union County Veterans Department. This history was inspired by numerous visits to the cemetery with my mother, the highlight of which was to see my grandmother's grave. As always, both of my parents, Robert and Mary Dunkerly, provided much support and gave the tour a 'test walk.'

Martha Wilson Headstone. Possibly the oldest in the cemetery, dated 1788.

1
Lewisburg, Port on the Susquehanna

For much of the Eighteenth Century, the wide, shallow Susquehanna River marked the frontier of colonial Pennsylvania. By the 1760s settlers were gradually approaching from the southeast. Families lived on isolated farms or in small settlements along the area's creeks and rivers.

What is now Union County was part of Northumberland County during the Revolutionary War period. Thus, residents of Lewisburg and Union County who fought against the British in that conflict were credited with service in the Northumberland County militia. The closing of the war in 1783 allowed for continued settlement in this region.

Founded in 1785, Lewisburg was first known as Derrstown, named for early resident Ludwig Derr. Derrstown's prosperity was tied to commerce on the Susquehanna River. The town was renamed Lewisburg in 1812, and the following year saw Union County created. New Berlin was the county seat for many years.[1]

The town followed a pattern of growth and development similar to that of many communities in the nation. The early decades of the Nineteenth Century saw a surge in transportation improvements: canals and roads, which hastened greater communication and commerce. The opening of the Lewisburg and Mifflinburg Turnpike in 1829 (modern Route 45) and the Eastern Division of the Pennsylvania Canal in 1833 brought prosperity to the town. Trade and commerce flourished. Later, the railroads overtook these modes of transportation, and connected the town to even more destinations.[2]

Lewisburg experienced prosperity, as much of the nation did, in the antebellum period. In the 1860s, the town sent many of its young men to fight in the Civil War. The growth of the University at Lewisburg (later Bucknell University) impacted the town by bringing gifted instructors and important community activists to the area. Three of the university's founders, Joseph Meixell, William H. Ludwig, and James Moore III, are buried in the cemetery.[3]

In 1869 the railroad arrived in Lewisburg, ushering new changes for the residents of Union County. Rail lines had been on the rise all across the state, with many running near the county.

Lewisburg finally became tied into the network after several earlier attempts to do so languished.[4]

The small town became tied to the golden age of baseball, with many stars of the early 1900s having played at Bucknell University. Four who went on to play in the wildly popular professional league were buried here in the cemetery.[5]

Large numbers of the town's men served in the World Wars during the Twentieth Century. Pioneers in science, medicine, and women's rights advanced their causes in the Twentieth Century as well.

By the close of the Twentieth Century, the Lewisburg Cemetery had become the resting place for many of the community's founders, defenders, leaders, promoters, and benefactors. A review of the cemetery, or better yet a walk through the grounds, reveals over two hundred years of history. The cemetery itself is an outdoor museum; open every day, yet a fragile one in need of constant care.

3
The Rise of Rural Cemeteries

Cemeteries reflect the history and culture of the communities of which they are an integral part. One author in fact has called them archaeological artifacts. In the late Eighteenth and early Nineteenth Century, family plots and church graveyards were typically the final resting place for the departed. Cemeteries were seldom visited except for funerals. This gradually changed during the Federal Period, after the American Revolution.[6]

The Nineteenth Century saw the rise of a new movement in funerary artwork, as people began to use elaborately decorated tombstones, monuments, and mausoleums. For those of the Victorian era, a cemetery was a place of reflection. Beginning in the 1830s, landscape designers began creating artwork in cemeteries. They were places to gather, visit the deceased, and enjoy the outdoors. Known as the Rural Cemetery Movement, municipal cemeteries became places of reflection and bastions of moral values. Sculpture, landscaping, and tombstones reflect this trend.[7]

City parks and cemeteries both grew in popularity during the late Nineteenth Century. Designed with natural features, they were places for the public to gather and enjoy ornamental gates, gardens, plantings, paths and drives. These pastoral landscapes, inspired by the rural cemeteries of the English Romantic style, were perfect locations for country picnics. The nation's first rural cemetery, Mount Auburn in Cambridge, Massachusetts, was established in 1831. During the 1830s and 1840s many American cities like Buffalo, Philadelphia, Boston, Baltimore, Richmond, Brooklyn, New York, Rochester, and others developed such parks and cemeteries.[8]

Inspired by Perce-Lachaise in Paris, rural cemeteries became places where visitors could stroll in quiet reflection while admiring the surrounding monuments and bucolic scenery. These locations were designed with graceful curves, open views, scenic plantings, and ornate architecture on headstones. Here Victorian Americans could connect with nature, get fresh air, and satisfy their desire for nostalgia and for a rural landscape, all in cities which were the antithesis of such places. It is no coincidence that the rural cemetery and park movements came into vogue at the same period that saw the rise of slums, tenements, and massive industrialization in the large cities of the United States.[9]

City cemeteries became places for Sunday strolls, family gatherings, and other social events. They were repositories for the values of morality, family, and Christianity. These cemeteries were perfect places for families to gather, spend time, enjoy picnics, and commune with the dead. The rising middle class families went to "visit their dead" in a manicured outdoor setting.[10]

The movement incorporated ideas about landscaping and design such as ornamental planting, winding roads, and tombstone sculpture. The movement coincided with the creation of urban parks and- after the Civil War- National Cemeteries, all of which shared similar features.[11]

Hand in hand with this movement was the development of elaborate mourning rituals. From viewings to home adornment to donning black clothing, Victorian Americans followed strict guidelines.

Death was a largely personal affair in the Nineteenth Century, and these new cemeteries reflected this thinking. Viewings were held at home, family members often prepared the body for burial, and locks of hair were typically saved as mementoes.[12]

Women especially followed strict rules that dictated how much black they wore and for how long. A women following the rules to the letter slowly emerged from this deep period of mourning, (anywhere from six months to two years), gradually shedding black layers as she appeared in public. Men frequently wore black armbands or other signs of mourning. Family members made mourning jewelry from locks of the deceased's hair.[13]

In time funeral rites moved to churches or other public gatherings and the science of morticians replaced the work done by family members at home. Gradually through the late 1800s, death became less personal and less of a family affair.[14]

Just as cemetery designs and mourning practices changed, so too did cemetery artwork. The designs and decorations on headstones and monuments are clues to its timeframe, and the mentality of the period. In the colonial period, motifs often included skulls, skeletons, hourglasses, and other symbolism suggesting life cut short. Carving headstones, usually of local material, was a skilled craft practiced by well trained carvers.[15]

In time, cemetery artwork became more elaborate, as the Victorian period adopted a sentimental and romantic view of death. Classical images became common, along with Gothic decorative features, angels, lions, lambs, urns, weeping willows, and others. Some of these suggested death as peaceful and anticipated an afterlife, others stressed innocence and sorrow.[16]

Another important cemetery tradition began at this time, in the nearby town of Boalsburg. In 1864 Emma Hunter and Sophie Keller placed flowers on the grave of Emma's father Reuben, killed during the Civil War. Feeling that none of the veterans should be neglected, they soon began placing flowers on the graves of others from the Civil War, Mexican War, and War of 1812. In time other ladies of the town joined them. The practice became known as Decoration Day, and was eventually formalized in 1868 as Memorial Day, held every May 30th.[17]

The founding of the Lewisburg Cemetery in 1848 coincided with the Rural Cemetery movement, and the cemetery displays many examples of funerary art. This burial ground was designed with a purposeful layout to allow residents of the town to visit their departed loved ones in a picturesque setting.

6
The Town Needs A Cemetery

By 1840, Lewisburg had grown rapidly from a population of 924 in 1830 to 2,042 in 1850. Its population doubled again between 1856 and 1868. The town was about to enter one of its most prosperous periods, with commerce, industry, education, and agriculture all flourishing. Many of the newcomers arrived from the southeastern part of the state, often from Philadelphia. In the town's early decades a large number of settlers of German heritage moved into the Susquehanna Valley.[18]

In the late 1840s when Lewisburg's residents began their city cemetery, several important issues faced residents of the town. News of the California Gold Rush dominated national headlines. War with Mexico had been raging for two years, yet the end was in sight. The town was having its own internal conflict as villagers argued over temperance. For time being, teetotalers won the vote.[19]

New Berlin was the county seat at the time the cemetery was established. In a vote to change the courthouse location, Lewisburg and Mifflinburg vied for the prize. Lewisburg won the contest in 1855 by just over 200 votes. It was decided that the new courthouse building "should be erected by the successful town, without any cost to the taxpayers."[20]

The crosscut canal, which ushered in a period of growth and prosperity, had opened in 1833. The canal connected Lewisburg to Montandon, and larger markets as far away as Philadelphia. Soon the telegraph arrived, linking the town to the outside world.[21]

In 1835 the town dedicated a monument to Colonel John Kelly, one of the area's early settlers and a veteran of the Revolution. The ceremony took place in the "English graveyard" at the Presbyterian Church and the local militia, along with the handful of surviving Revolutionary veterans, participated. General Abbott Green was Grand Marshall. It was an elaborate funeral procession, not to be exceeded until that of Colonel James Cameron in 1862.[22]

More and more of the town's Revolutionary War veterans were also passing during these early decades of the Nineteenth Century. They had become eligible for pensions in 1832, and many gathered at the county courthouse in New Berlin to file their paperwork. These men, mostly in their seventies and eighties, had witnessed the growth of Union County and widespread prosperity. As they, and the community's founding generation passed on, many were laid to rest in cemeteries across the county or at various places in Lewisburg.[23]

Until 1848, Lewisburg residents used small cemeteries located at the intersection of Third Street and Market, and Fifth and Market. As in many communities across the nation in the early nineteenth century, soon the church graveyards were not large enough to accommodate the growing population. Lewisburg, like other towns, needed a city cemetery, not tied to a religious group.[24]

Both the Presbyterian and Lutheran Churches also had small graveyards in the village before the establishment of the city cemetery. The burials from these cemeteries were moved to the new Lewisburg cemetery after it opened. The *Union County Times*, published in New Berlin, listed deaths, but not where the deceased were buried.[25]

While Lewisburg was known as Derrstown in the 1790s, Presbyterian residents had to travel four miles to Buffalo Crossroads to worship at the church there. Yet they bought lots in the town along Market Street and established a Presbyterian cemetery there. The First Presbyterian Church, built in 1832-3, was predated by the cemetery.[26]

On April 10th of 1848, prominent citizens formed the Lewisburg Cemetery Association, and purchased six acres from John Chamberlain "west of the limit of the borough." A boundary tree still stands (in 2013) to mark the old town limit. The acreage was divided into 1,065 plots for purchase.[27]

With the creation of a town cemetery, graves from the various churches were transferred to the new location. Yet not all were moved. The grave of William Wilson, for example, is under the steps of the Presbyterian Church. His tombstone, and that of his son Francis, was relocated to the Wilson plot of the cemetery. The grave and monument of Colonel John Kelly were among those removed to the new cemetery.[28]

Several early headstones reflect artwork of the time, including those of General Abbott Green and Colonel William Chamberlin. Both of these prominent men have tombstones which are good examples of cemetery symbolism.

Green markers. The open book represents the bible, and their faith.[29]

Chamberlin Stone. The wreath represents victory over death.[30]

In 1849 the Association oversaw construction of a Sexton's House on Seventh Street. It stood in the cemetery, directly across from the intersection with St. Catherine Street. George J. Roland was the cemetery's first sexton. Next was George Donachy, who recorded the internments and oversaw the maintenance of the grounds.[31]

Lewisburg's earlier burials took place at the various churches that had been established throughout the town up to that time. In 1833 the German Reformed Lutheran Church was organized at Church and Third Street. That same year the Methodist Church was consecrated at the same intersection. The next year the German Presbyterian Church gave privileges for burials in the German Burying Ground to the Lutheran Church. In 1851 the Lutherans bought out the interests of the German Reformed Church at St Louis and Third Street.[32]

This "German Cemetery" would be used for only fifteen years. When the city cemetery opened in 1848, graves were removed from the German Cemetery to the new city graveyard. The German Cemetery was located at the present site of the brownstone sanctuary.[33]

George F. Miller served as the Cemetery Association's first President until his death in 1885. Miller was a judge and United States congressman, and actively worked to organize the group. He also wrote the Act of Incorporation, and donated money for the purchase of the grounds. Miller actively promoted railroads, finally seeing the arrival of rails in the town. The next two Presidents were Thomas Beaver and J. Thompson Baker. Other officers in the new organization included Treasurer Thomas Hayes, Secretary William Wilson, and Managers Samuel Wolfe, James P. Ross, James Moore Jr., Solomon Ritter, Levi B. Christ, John Chamberlain, Henry Noll, Dr. William Hayes, Levi Sterner, Hugh P. Sheller, Stephen S. Lyndall, Peter Nevius, Flavel Clingan, John Gundy, and Jacob Gundy.[34]

According to one history of the town, "The site for the cemetery could not have been better selected. It is on a gently inclining hill overlooking the town and the way it is laid out in neat avenues, and the number of trees that have been planted and are now large enough to cast abundant shade, make this cemetery really one of the most beautiful to be found in the state." Thus, contemporaries saw it as part of the growing rural cemeteries appearing across the country.[35]

The first burial was made on November 2nd, 1848 for Ogden A. Barnes, son of John and Katharine Barnes. He is buried in section 1, and was moved here from another cemetery. The oldest headstone in the cemetery is that of Martha Wilson, who died November 29, 1788. Her remains were also moved from another burying ground.[36]

Beginning the fall of 1848 and lasting on until the next year, graves were systematically removed from the town's two church cemeteries: the Presbyterian and Lutheran, and relocated to the Lewisburg Cemetery. Some graves also came from Buffalo Crossroads Church. Graves were still being moved as late as 1852. Moving graves, or even entire cemeteries, was not uncommon in the Nineteenth Century.[37]

The cemetery was founded during an important decade, a generation was passing and Lewisburg, and the nation, were changing in fundamental ways. Revolutionary veterans, the valley's early settlers, and early town leaders were passing and a second generation of native born residents was taking the helm. Lewisburg, Pennsylvania, and the nation were also entering a prosperous period of economic growth.

Thomas Beaver of Danville, second president of the Association, contributed $500 for the iron fence that borders the cemetery along Seventh Street. Wire fences enclosed the site on the other three sides. Beaver also funded a fountain on the cemetery's Second Avenue.[38]

The Lewisburg Cemetery was originally laid out with a series of Avenues and circular plots. The main entrance was located at the intersection with St Catherine and Seventh Street. The main avenue entering the cemetery ran about 100 yards then circled a plot in the middle of the street. Two other circular plots broke up the main road running in from Seventh Street. These were occupied by prominent families including Warrens, Kremers, Christs, Shrivers, Williams, Millers, and Brights.

Other landscaping features included benches "in convenient places." A square was set aside for Union veterans, now the Veterans Section near the current main entrance. Grand Army of the Republic Post 52 (an organization of Union Civil War veterans) was given charge of this area for the town's Civil War dead.[39]

Headstone with hand pointing upward. This symbol, common in the mid to late 1800s, represented hope of heaven and afterlife.

The 1850s saw the passing of another generation in the Susquehanna Valley. Many first generation Lewisburg and Union County residents had passed on. By 1854 the cemetery had 254 burials, of which 124 were transfers.[40]

In 1861 the town saw many of its young men march off to put down the Rebellion, now known as the Civil War. The conflict created an entire generation of military veterans. Men and women from Union County saw action in many areas of the war, and were present at most of the major battles.

Seven Kline brothers fought in the war, a remarkable contribution by this family, with five serving in Company E of the 51st Pennsylvania. One of them, Reuben, is buried here in the cemetery.[41]

Many Lewisburg and area residents defended their home state at Gettysburg. Men from several Pennsylvania units fought in the battle's first day, when Union forces were overwhelmed by larger numbers of Confederates. Andrew G. Tucker is one of the town's more prominent Gettysburg casualties. Another was a Captain in the same regiment, John A. Owens.

The war created new opportunities for women, and one of the fields that they entered was nursing. Several Lewisburg women served in the war as nurses, being stationed at different points in the South. Annabella Vorse Clark tended to the wounded in Union-occupied Nashville during the war.[42]

Veterans Section

In the veterans section, amid a sea of American flags, stands a lone Confederate flag. It flies over the grave of John W. Jordan of Virginia. From Staunton, Virginia, he was a hotel owner before the war. He enlisted at the start of the war in 1861. Information on his military service is sketchy and conflicting. After the war he came to Lewisburg as an itinerant merchant, where he died on August 22, 1867. He was buried "with honors due a fighting man, regardless of which flag he served under, by the Grand Army of the Republic (a Union veterans organization)."[43]

Jordan Grave

One of the more prominent Civil War deaths from the town was that of Colonel James Cameron. He was killed in the first major battle of the war, at Manassas (Bull Run), Virginia in 1861.

After being buried twice near Manassas, Virginia, Colonel James Cameron's remains were finally recovered by Union troops and brought to Pennsylvania. Battlefield burials, often done hastily and in the presence of enemy forces, were usually poorly done and marked with only wooden headboards. In Washington the remains were placed in a coffin. On March 17, 1862, a military escort from the War Department brought the coffin to Lewisburg, stopping first at the state capital.

James Cameron Grave

Slifer Marker

Joining them in Harrisburg was Secretary of the Commonwealth Eli Slifer, along with several members from the state Legislature and House of Representatives. The party reached Lewisburg after midnight, and proceeded to the home of James's brother William Cameron. A detachment of soldiers from the 54th Pennsylvania stood guard over the remains through the night.[44]

The next day the family had a private religious service, followed by a procession through the streets of Lewisburg to the cemetery. A large crowd gathered along the sidewalks to pay their respects. The funeral procession included the hearse drawn by four white horses, a military honor guard, A.L. Russell, the Adjutant General of Pennsylvania, Secretary of the Commonwealth Eli Slifer, R.C. Hale, the state's Quartermaster General, and even a handful of War of 1812 veterans. At 1 p.m. Reverend P. Rizer of Sunbury gave the eulogy at the graveside and Bucknell President Justin Loomis gave an address.[45]

The *Lewisburg Chronicle* noted that, "business generally was suspended, and the line of procession, the windows and some roofs, were thronged with spectators." It was possibly the most elaborate funeral in Lewisburg's history.[46]

The Civil War had another lasting impact on Lewisburg and Union County through the establishment of Decoration Day. In the years following the conflict, local chapters of the G.A.R. took the lead in promoting the effort to decorate the graves of fallen Civil War soldiers. In 1868 the *Lewisburg Chronicle* published orders from G.A.R. commander General John A. Logan, stating that "The 30th day of May, 1868, is designated for the purpose of strewing with flowers or otherwise decorating the graves of comrades who died in defense of their country during the late rebellion, and whose bodies now lie in almost every city, village and hamlet churchyard in the land. In this observance, no form of ceremony is prescribed, but posts and comrades will in their own way arrange such fitting services and testimonials of respect as circumstances may permit."[47]

The first Decoration Day observance drew about fifty G.A.R. members that year. The tradition continues today, now known as Memorial Day.[48]

Following the war were several decades of prosperity for Union County. The nation received a shock in the summer of 1876 when a force of cavalry under General George A. Custer met disaster at the hands of the Sioux on the Little Bighorn River. The country had been basking in its Centennial, with a major exposition underway in Philadelphia. Amid all the pageantry and optimism of the Centennial, news of the defeat on the frontier was astounding. Among those serving with cavalry that day was

Wilbur Blair. A Civil War veteran, he survived the Battle of Little Bighorn, and rests in the Lewisburg Cemetery.

Thirty years after its creation, the cemetery was nearing its capacity, so the Association purchased an additional six acres from Jones Geddens in 1878.[49]

Mourning practices were changing at this time. By the 1880s the mortuary science had developed more fully, and funerals become more mainstream, allowing for the deceased to be prepared for funerals by professionals. Up to this point, death had been largely a family affair, with the body prepared by relatives, and viewings held at home. Now this process moved out of the house to a more public space. Embalming became the rule, rather than the exception.[50]

Mourning practices for the family included women wearing black for long periods of time, and gradually shedding black in their day to day clothing over time. Widows who strictly adhered to the custom would wear black for two years. The term casket, rather than coffin, became widely used, referring to a container for precious relics or objects. Death, like many other aspects of Victorian life, was sentimental. This was reflected in the artwork found on markers and headstones put up at the time. The next few examples will illustrate this trend.[51]

One of Lewisburg's most prominent citizens in the late 1800s was James Merrill Linn. He joined the Union army at the outbreak of the Civil War, serving with other Lewisburg men in the 4th Pennsylvania (a three month regiment). He was a successful lawyer, educator, and historian.

James Merrill Linn grave.

The Lewisburg cemetery's roads were macadamized by the 1890s, providing a measure of stability and firmness in bad weather. The Cemetery Association and the Tucker Post of the Grand Army of the Republic (Union veterans of the Civil War) reserved a space for military veterans along the Seventh Street side of the graveyard. Many Civil War veterans were buried here, and in time were joined by service members from later conflicts.

By 1898 there were 3,860 graves in the cemetery. The Association used money collected from plot purchases to maintain the grounds.[52]

Foster Grave. The crown represents glory in the afterlife, the cross symbolizes faith.

Enna Foster Grave. Example of intricate detail on some markers. Note classical columns and wreath.

Geddes Monument, with angel representing afterlife.

In 1899 the Cemetery Association built a Gothic Chapel at the eastern end of the grounds. Constructed of dark red brownstone, it is near the main entrance off of Seventh Street. When construction started in May, the association decided to place a time capsule. In a box above the front door are three copies of the cemetery charter, a copy of the *Lewisburg Saturday News*, one of the *Lewisburg Chronicle*, two of the *Lewisburg Journal*, one of the *Philadelphia Press*, and statements from the First National Bank and the Union National Bank of Lewisburg. Behind the chapel, built at the same time, was a stone vault.[53]

The building committee included J. Thompson Baker, A.W. Brown, J.W. VanValzah, C. F. Lindig, and William Jones. The stone contractor was Chauncey Foster and the project's carpenter was William Yoder. Both rest here in the cemetery they helped create.[54]

Apparently the grounds were maintained by Donald Donachy, son of the cemetery's sexton George. In July of that year, Donald was cutting grass when he ran the point of a cycle into his ankle, "inflicting a very painful wound." Another son, William succeeded George as the next Sexton in 1894.[55]

Chapel

Chapel

Near the current main entrance there is a gatehouse with a belfry, believed to be associated with the original Sexton's Home. The home was moved across the street and is now part of Bucknell's campus. The Cemetery's governing board appointed Henry Noll to place a shrubbery in front of the building. Noll traveled to Philadelphia in order to get a quality product. Upon completion, thieves dug up the plantings, and Noll offered a reward for their arrest. Whether justice was ever served remains unknown.[56]

Sexton's House, now across the street from the cemetery entrance.

Gatehouse

In the late 1800s a new type of headstone appeared in American cemeteries, and quickly caught on as trendy. The material, known as white bronze, is actually pure zinc. From a distance it resembles stone, though closer examination reveals it is clearly metal. Hollow monuments and headstones, made of this new material, rose on cemeteries across the nation.[57]

They soon lost favor, however, as many continued to prefer traditional stone as the material for burials and monuments. Within about forty years, use of zinc declined. The Lewisburg cemetery has several excellent examples of this type of material, many with intricate detail.[58]

Mary Williams Marker, an example of a White Bronze, or Zinc, marker. The broken rose represents young life cut short. Roses were common on women's or girls' graves.

Example of White Bronze, or Zinc, marker.

The cemetery continued to be an important gathering place for community groups. In July of 1899, members of the William Cameron Engine Company decorated the graves of firefighters who rested in the cemetery.[59]

An article from the *Lewisburg Chronicle* that year exemplifies the traditional Memorial Day programs held in the cemetery at the time. The Tucker Post of the Grand Army of the Republic (Union Civil War veterans) gathered at their hall and led a procession that included the town's fire department, Knights of the Golden Eagle, Patriotic Order of the Sons of America, and private citizens. From Fourth and Market Street, the line moved to Front Street, then back to Market to Seventh, and finally entered the cemetery.[60]

The G.A.R. members decorated the graves of veterans, and the day included music and a benediction. Other local G.A.R. posts participated in the event. William Gretzinger of Bucknell University delivered the main address, noting that "These graves contain the dust of heroes." Memorial Day observances held up through the 1930s and 40s, when Civil War veterans still participated, must have been particularly compelling.[61]

Also at the turn of the century, Lewisburg's Daughters of the American Revolution chapter began an effort to record the names of all Revolutionary War soldiers in the county. They hoped to "save from oblivion" the graves of these men.[62]

The language used by various civic and patriotic groups in describing the cemetery's importance and its role in the community are found in the words they used to describe the graveyard. It was a "Sleeping places of the Dead" and visiting the site was an "honored privilege" for the townspeople. Memorial Day in particular was a "sacred obligation" and was a "pilgrimage to the silent cities of the dead." Lastly, in the tradition of Victorian cemeteries, it was a place to commune with nature and with loved ones, a "Beautifully solemn scene."[63]

Lewisburg continued to grow and make internal improvements during these decades. During the last decade of the Nineteenth Century the town paved its streets, expanded its sewer lines, and installed incandescent street lights. Those living through the turn of the century saw astounding improvements in their lives.

In the 1890s three remarkable women graduated from Bucknell University, and became known as the "Three Marys." Two of them are buried in the cemetery. Mary Belle Harris launched an impressive career in prisons, where she promoted humane treatment of inmates. She is buried in the northwestern section of the cemetery.[64]

Mary Moore Wolfe attended medical school after Bucknell and worked with mentally ill patients at various institutions. She founded the Village for Feebleminded Women at Laurelton, a cutting- edge institution at the time.[65]

Mary Moore Wolfe Grave

Lastly, Mary Bartol studied languages at Bucknell, and later in graduate school. She taught classical languages at Rockford College in Illinois. After marrying Bucknell graduate Lewis E. Theiss, they returned to Lewisburg, however they are not buried here.[66]

In 1905 the cemetery expanded, adding a new section to the west. A few years later in 1913 construction was underway at the Lutheran Church to build a new parsonage when workers stumbled upon graves. Apparently they were burials from the old cemetery, and been missed when graves were transferred to the city cemetery. A total of six graves were recovered at this time.[67]

As the town marked the passage of the Nineteenth Century, another generation was passing. Civil War veterans were dying off, though many lived on until the 1940s and 50s. Bucknell University was a well-established institution with national recognition. Those born in the Nineteenth Century would cross the century mark as the town entered the 1900s. Automobiles and trucks soon replaced horses and wagons along the city's streets.

The first decades of the Twentieth Century were, in many ways, the golden age of baseball. The sport had become immensely popular, and the two professional organizations, the National and American Leagues, played a championship game in 1903 known as the World Series. Baseball clubs sprung up all over the country: in workplaces, churches, and social clubs. Bucknell University attracted many athletes, and its baseball teams featured many outstanding players. This trend is reflected in the presence of several outstanding players, buried in the cemetery. Most had connections to Bucknell University.[68]

Another Bucknell connection was Charles Bell, who worked at the University for over forty years. Born a slave in Romney, Virginia (now West Virginia), he escaped to Pennsylvania and then went onto Canada before the outbreak of the Civil War. While passing through Lewisburg after the war, he was noted by University President James Looms and hired to work on the campus grounds. Bell was known for his hard work and was admired by the university's managers. He died in 1912 and rests in an unmarked grave in the cemetery.[69]

By 1918 World War One had raged for four years in Europe, and America was finally caught up in the struggle. Pennsylvanians found themselves in Europe as part of the American military effort. Many Union County men joined the 103rd Trench Mortar Battalion and departed for France. On September 26, 1918, a German shell hit an ammunition dump amid the men of the 103rd Trench Mortar Battalion in the Argonne Forest in France. Killed were Sergeant Edward Shannon, Ralph J. Dull, Bright L. Kratzer, Leon C. Pierce, Robert D. Rimert, and Bromley Smith. Lewisburg's American Legion Post would be named Kratzer-Dull in honor of two of these men. They were initially interred in France, and brought home for burial in Lewisburg in 1921.[70]

Dull Grave

Yost Grave

Colonel Henry Spyker, another World War I soldier, is buried in France, but has a marker here in the Lewisburg cemetery. Another soldier from the Great War (as it was first called), was Christopher Mathewson. Better known as an incredible athlete, Mathewson attended Bucknell University and was a skilled baseball pitcher. In 1936 he was one of the first inductees into the Baseball Hall of Fame in Cooperstown, New York. During the war Mathewson served in the chemical corps, and was exposed to poisonous gas that the Germans used against the Americans. His lungs were damaged and never fully recovered.[71]

For the rest of his life, despite being unable to play, Mathewson was seen as one of the great heroes of professional baseball. He served in the organization in a variety of capacities, promoting the game and being an ambassador for the sport. He died in 1925, one of the most respected players of the game.[72]

Mathewson Plot

Another World War I soldier, and athlete, found here is Harry "Moose" McCormick. He played baseball with New York, Pittsburgh, and Philadelphia. During the World War he volunteered and achieved the rank of Captain. Later he coached baseball and basketball at Bucknell. He married Lewisburg native Dorothy Walls, and lived his remaining years here.[73]

McCormick Grave

Shortly after the closing of the Great War, as it was known, Lewisburg residents such as Mary Moore Wolfe and other local women achieved an important victory of their own: suffrage. In 1920 the XIX Amendment was ratified, guaranteeing all Americans the right to vote. Two years later, the cemetery grew again, adding more land to the west.[74]

There were other important changes in the early decades of the Twentieth Century as well. Telephones became more common, automobiles were gradually replacing horses on the town's streets, and homes were using electricity for cooking and light, rather than stoves or fireplaces.

Seventy years after its founding, the first attempt at documenting the names in the cemetery was undertaken by Martha A. Bartol, historian of the Shikelimo Chapter of the Daughters of the American Revolution. From 1919-1924 she diligently recorded the names on the headstones, and was able to note which burials had been transferred from the town's other cemeteries (primarily the Presbyterian and Lutheran, but some also were relocated from Buffalo Crossroads Church). This first attempt to document the names of those who rest in the cemetery, and its early history, has been an invaluable resource for those who came later.[75]

    The Second World War had a major impact on Lewisburg and Union County. The citizens of the Buffalo Valley supported the war through various methods, including scrap drives, buying bonds, and serving in the military. More World War II veterans rest in the cemetery than from any other conflict. Not all came back: a World War II soldier who died overseas and rests in a military cemetery there is Fred Getz. Just after the conflict, in 1946, the cemetery was expanded for the last time.[76]

Getz Marker

Lewisburg, like much of the nation, enjoyed tremendous prosperity in the postwar years. A Memorial Day observance from 1948 illustrates the continued importance of the cemetery in town life. A parade left the Kratzer-Dull American Legion Post and moved down Market Street to Seventh Street. Veterans and school children decorated the graves of veterans.
   The procession included the Lewisburg High School Band, Spanish-American War veterans, Veterans of Foreign Wars, the American Legion, and other patriotic groups.[77]
   Preservation of the cemetery's headstones has been a constant concern for area residents. In 1948 Staunton "Uby" Kohler initiated a project to repair the twenty Civil War headstones in the Veterans section which had become hard to read. The Lewisburg Memorial Works agreed to do the work at cost. The Kratzer-Dull V.F.W. Post contributed funding to the project. Names were in danger of being lost, and had this critical work not been done, important information may have been forever lost.[78]
   In the 1990s, First Presbyterian Church on Market Street launched an expansion, and construction uncovered an unknown grave, illustrating that not all burials were moved when the city

cemetery opened fifty years earlier. The remains were removed to the cemetery.[79]

The Lewisburg Cemetery reflects several historic periods, including the town's early settlers and promoters, the Rural Cemetery movement, Victorian cemetery art, Civil War burials, and various changes in cemetery art. Studying those who rest here reveals the prominent intuitions, such as churches and social clubs, as well as important industries, like the stores, canals, railroads, and educational centers, that comprised Lewisburg's past.

Here are seen the numerous family connections among the town's prominent citizens. The community's early leaders often intermarried, and many of them founded its first institutions like the early churches. Later, other leading citizens founded Bucknell University and served as trustees and faculty. Civil War veterans formed the Tucker Post of the Grand Army of the Republic, and promoted the Memorial Day tradition of decorating graves. Each generation has made its contribution to the town's history, and has left its imprint on the cemetery. The burying ground today is a composite of these various generations and their values.

In 2004 the latest attempt to record the names in the cemetery was undertaken by Sam Alcorn. He built on the earlier work done by Martha Bartol, finding that many of the names she recorded in the 1920s were illegible eighty years later.

As Union County reaches its 200th Anniversary, the cemetery is an important place to reflect on the community's past and its accomplishments. Storm damage in the summer of 2011 forced the removal of several old trees here, there are plans for new landscaping in this area.

The Cemetery Association continues to oversee the care of the grounds and look towards the future. The cemetery plans to add space for cremations near the chapel, possibly adding up to fifteen more columbiums. A new fountain, expanded walkway, and more landscaping will complete this expansion.[80]

Cemetery Tour

This walking tour journeys through the cemetery's early years and past its most prominent burials. The walk takes about an hour and is generally arranged in a chronological order. Be sure to wear good walking shoes, the ground is uneven and you will be on gravel, pavement, and grass at various times.

Take your time and enjoy the cemetery. Be sure to look around as you walk and search for interesting graves and artwork beyond those mentioned in the tour. You never know when you will learn something new about Union County or make a connection.

Begin at the entrance and walk out to Seventh Street and turn left, and proceed to the DAR Marker and Oak tree.

1. Witness Tree

This oak is from the 1789 land survey that marked the western boundary of the town of Lewisburg. It is a tangible link to the town's founding. Walk back to the entrance, turn into the cemetery, and pause at the Veterans Section.[81]

Oak Marker

2. Veterans Section
Established in the 1880s, this section features two Civil War mortars and a number of veterans from that and later conflicts. The cemetery's lone Confederate, a soldier from Virginia, rests here in the front row. At Memorial Day all of the headstones have flags, and a Confederate flag flies over the lone southerner. The cemetery's founders set this area aside to be used by members of the local GAR Post (Grand Army of the Republic).

Each military conflict has a distinct plaque which is placed at the headstone of the veteran. These are visible throughout the cemetery, make a note of them. For example, the Revolutionary veteran's marker has a Minuteman, Civil War burials are indicated by a GAR marker, Spanish-American War soldiers have a cross shaped plaque. In later parts of the cemetery you will see World War I, II, Korea, and Vietnam markers. There are only a handful of War of 1812, Mexican War, and Spanish-American War veterans here. Consider yourself lucky if you spot one.

Along the way you may also notice other, non- military plaques for firefighters, and various organizations like the Daughters of the American Revolution, Knights of Columbus, and other fraternal and community association.

From here proceed over to the Chapel and pause in front of it.

World War I Marker

3. Chapel

Built in 1899, the stone chapel is used for events and special occasions. The Gothic style architecture was popular at the time of its construction, similar in design to many of the town's churches. Behind you note the Columbarium (for cremations) and fountain. Future plans call for the expansion of this area and more landscaping. Return to the main road, turn right, and walk a short distance uphill. Himmelreich's impressive marker will be on the left just beyond the Veterans Section.[82]

4. William D. Himmelreich

William D. Himmelreich donated money to establish the first library in Lewisburg. His generosity was reflected in naming the library after him when it stood next to the Presbyterian Church in downtown Lewisburg. His monument is built to resemble a Greek temple with columns, likely in recognition of his passion for education.

Look past the Himmelreich monument and notice the mausoleum on the edge of the cemetery property. This is the resting place of Walter Blair, Bucknell baseball player who also played in the major leagues. If you chose, you may walk over to see this. From the current stop, walk past the Himmelriech monument, and stop at the plain tall shaft for the Focht family.

William D. Himmelreich Grave

5. Benjamin Focht

Best known as the "Father of Old Age Pensions," Focht was active in local, state and national politics in the early Twentieth Century. He was editor and publisher of Lewisburg's *Saturday News* in the 1880s. He then served in both the state Senate and the U.S. Congress. He promoted retirement pensions while in office. Focht wrote of his town, "I learned character in Lewisburg, and what I learned prepared me to defend my views . . ." From here walk further uphill to the first intersection with the Path of Friendship (not a paved road, but grass). Turn right and walk down the path, passing by the Chapel on your right. At the second telephone pole, turn left and walk into the section to find a tall brownstone marker for Justin Loomis.[83]

Focht Monumnet

6. Justin Loomis

First President of Bucknell University, he guided the school through the difficult Civil War years. Loomis served in this capacity from 1858-79 and oversaw construction of the President's home on campus. In July, 1863 he took university faculty to the Gettysburg battlefield to search for wounded Lewisburg residents. Gettysburg will figure prominently as the tour proceeds: it was the largest battle of the war, the only major engagement fought in Pennsylvania, and many area troops fought there.

Now turn left (north as you face the marker) and continue walking the same direction as you were on Serenity Lane, for about fifty feet to the Kelly Monument, a white marker with a pointed top.

7. Kelly Marker

Perhaps one of the most famous residents of the cemetery, Col. John Kelly was an early settler and soldier who fought in the Revolution. Originally buried at the Presbyterian (English) Church on Market Street, Kelly's remains were moved here when the cemetery opened. His, along with that of William Cameron, was one of the most elaborate funerals in Lewisburg's history.

Next proceed over to the lane on your left as you face the Kelly marker with Seventh Street behind it, and pause at the avenue. Look to the right to discern a circle of burials in the avenue ahead of you. It may take a moment to discern the circle. Study it and look uphill to your left to see two other circles.

8. Original Designs Features

Here note the original layout of the cemetery, with three circles along what was the main avenue. Looking to the east, towards Seventh Street, reveals the site of the original cemetery entrance. This rise of ground was where the cemetery started, before expanding north and west. Continue west (uphill), passing the next two circles, and look for the Linn family plot on your right, just beyond the third circle. There are four flat stones for the Linn family.

View of original Main Avenue

9. James Merrill Linn
Linn taught Latin and Greek at Franklin and Marshall College and later was an attorney in Lewisburg. He briefly served in the Civil War in 1861. His brother John Blair Linn wrote <u>Annals of Buffalo Valley, Pennsylvania</u>, an important book on area history.

James M. Linn photo. Courtesy of Ronn Palm.

From here look for the Green graves, farther up the hill on the right. They are both thin markers with open Bibles prominently carved onto the tombstones. You will approach them from the rear, so proceed carefully; you may have to turn around once or twice to see them.

10. Abbott Green

Son of a Revolutionary soldier and early settler in the valley, Green became one of the town's most influential residents. As an engineer he oversaw the construction of the Pennsylvania Canal in the 1830s. Its impact on the town cannot be overstated, it jump started Lewsiburg's ante bellum prosperity. Green was active in organizing the Presbyterian Church in Lewisburg and Bucknell University. He was also a general in the state's militia. Proceed further up the path and watch for the Tucker monument, sitting directly on the side of the road.

11. Andrew Gregg Tucker

The first Bucknell graduate to die in the Civil War, he was a Lieutenant of the 142nd Pennsylvania. Tucker died on the first day of the battle of Gettysburg on July 1, 1863, defending his home state. Lewisburg's Grand Army of the Republic Post (organization of Union Veterans) was named in his honor. Next is the prominent Cameron family plot, straight back behind Tucker's grave.

Before turning in from the avenue, note that you are in the heart of the most prominent part of the old cemetery. Surrounding you are the area's founders and its movers and shakers from the Nineteenth Century. If you wish, take time to look for the Meixells, Chamberlins, McClures and others who are nearby.

12. Cameron Family

The Camerons were a prominent family and several notable individuals rest here. Each of their stones are elaborately decorated. William Cameron donated a steam engine and hoses to in 1875 to the town's fire department and it bears his name today. Colonel James Cameron fought in the Civil War, and fell at the Battle of First Manassas, Virginia in 1861- the first Pennsylvanian killed in the war. He was initially buried on the battlefield in a hastily dug grave. Not until Union troops could reclaim the body months later was he brought home to rest here. His funeral was one of the most elaborate in the town's history.[84]

Nearby rests another prominent Lewisburg family, the Slifers. Their plot is the next stop, just yards away.

13. Slifer Family

Eli Slifer aided Governor Andrew Curtin during the Civil War, serving as Secretary of the Commonwealth. A contemporary called him one of the "great men of Pennsylvania." He played a key role in running Pennsylvania's war effort during the Civil War- a state that was the second most populous in the Union and having important industrial and railroad facilities for the north's war effort. Today his home is open to the public as Slifer House Museum.

From this stop walk directly over to a marker for Harry McCormick. It is immediately adjacent to the Slifers.

14. Harry "Moose" McCormick

Moose played baseball for the New York Giants, Philadelphia Athletics, and Pittsburgh Pirates. He played in two World Series with the Giants, both of which they lost. For a period, McCormick and Christy Mathewson were teammates with the Giants. McCormick was the first pinch hitter in professional baseball. He married Lewisburg native Dorothy Walls, granddaughter of Eli Slifer and a Bucknell Graduate. Harry coached the Bucknell baseball and basketball teams from 1922-25. He later served as Director of Housing for the University.

McCormick Marker

From here walk directly back to the edge of the cemetery and look for two military headstones. These are the small, white markers found in National Cemeteries.

15. United States Colored Troops
Here along the edge of the cemetery rest two African Americans who fought in the Civil War: William and Milton Airey. William served in the 24th United States Colored Troops, stationed in Maryland and Virginia, while William was with the 40th United States Colored Troops, seeing action in Tennessee. Lewisburg has always had a small African American population. It is not known if these men were natives of the area or moved here, or how they are related (if at all).[85]

Next, turn left (as you face these markers) and walk up along the edge of the cemetery until you reach the next road, the Path of Peace. Look for a small marker with a flag, that of Ralph Dull.

His grave is about twenty feet from the intersection on the right side.

16. Ralph Dull
One of Lewisburg's World War I soldiers who died in France in an attack that killed several area men. The American Legion Post in Lewisburg is named after Kratzer and Dull, two of the soldiers killed at the same time. Elsewhere in the cemetery are others who were killed at the same time, as well as some who survived. The incident graphically illustrates the impact on a small town when National Guard units fight overseas.

From here walk further up the avenue you are on, the Path of Peace, to the next intersection, with Serenity Drive. Turn right and walk toward Route 15. Along the way you will be in a newer section of the cemetery. Note the dates and changes in styles in this later section. You will now be looking for a tall monument for the Harris family.

17. John Howard Harris
President of Bucknell from 1889-1919, professor of Philosophy, Trustee, and Civil War veteran, Harris was also a Baptist minister.

Across the road note a few burials from the 1810s, this is another early section of the cemetery.. As you walk from here you may note the grave of William W. Grove on your left, a survivor of the attack that killed Kratzer and Dull in 1918. Your next stop is further up Serenity Drive. Cross the next intersection (the Path of Rest) and shortly on your left you will see a large unique stone for the Fetherstons.

18. Edith Fetherston
Edith and her husband John were artists who settled in Lewisburg in a home near the bridge on Market Street. She willed her home to become a museum, now known as Packwood House. It is named after an ancestral home in England. The distinctive stone stands out, reflecting her talents as an artist.

Turn around and walk back to the Path of Rest, turning right. Walk to the next paved intersection at St George Drive, and turn left. This is the main entrance road into the cemetery. On your right watch for a flat marker for George Ramer, the cemetery's only Medal of Honor recipient. It is about fifty feet before you reach the intersection with the Path of Love, and about fifteen feet off the road.

Fetherston Grave

19. George Ramer
Awarded the Medal of Honor for his actions in the Korean War, he is the only medal recipient in the cemetery. Perhaps it is

appropriate that a soldier from the Korean War- often called the nation's forgotten conflict- is the cemetery's only recipient of this high honor. Ramer was born in Meyersdale in Western Pennsylvania, but moved to Lewisburg and graduated from High School here. He served in the navy during the later part of World War II. He later taught at both the High School and Bucknell University before re-entering military service.[86]

Now walk to the intersection with the Path of Love and turn left. Christy Matthewson's grave is about thirty feet on your left.

Ramer Grave

20. Christy Mathewson
Mathewson was an incredible athlete and promoter of baseball in the 1910s and 20s. He attended Bucknell, and went on to play

professionally for several teams. Exposure to poison gas in World War I damaged his lungs and he eventually succumbed to the effects. He rests here next to his wife and son, a veteran of World War II.

From here continue down the lane and look for the Wolfe family plot on your left.

21. Mary Moore Wolfe

One of the "Three Marys" of Bucknell, Mary M. Wolfe was a pioneer for women in the field of medicine. A graduate of Bucknell, she worked in thee Women's Division of the Norristown State Hospital for the Insane. Later she became the first superintendent of the Pennsylvania Village for Feeble Minded Women at Laurelton. She was also active in the movement for women's suffrage. From here proceed back to St. George Drive and return to your vehicle.

Of course, every grave has a story to tell. The tour highlights the famous, but each person resting in the cemetery made their own contributions to Lewisburg and Union County's history.

Notable Burials

Blair, Walter Allen "Heavy"
October 13, 1883- August 20, 1948

A native of Arnot, he played baseball at Bucknell University before joining the Major Leagues in 1907 at age 23. He played catcher with the New York Highlanders and Buffalo Buffeds. He also managed the Buffalo team until it folded. Following this he coached baseball at the University of Pittsburgh and at Bucknell. He joined the Bucknell Hall of Fame in 1987. He was a member of the First Presbyterian Church.[87]

Blair, Wilbur
-October 2, 1891

A musician during the Civil War, Blair served in the 7th Cavalry on the western plains afterward. He survived the Battle of Little Bighorn in 1876.

Brady, John and Mary.
John   1733-April 11, 1779
Mary   1735-October 20, 1783

John Brady was an early settler who was active in political and military affairs when the Susquehanna River was the frontier. He served as militia officer, jurist, surveyor, and . The Bradys lived near present day Montandon. During the Revolution he served as a captain commanding Company D of the 12th Pennsylvania. Brady was wounded at Brandywine in 1777. He returned to the frontier, organized local defenses, and built a fort at modern Muncy. Indians allied to the British ambushed and killed John in 1779. Mary Quigley married John at age 20 and moved to the frontier with him. She was born and raised in Cumberland County. After John's death she settled, with her young children, near modern Smoketown. Mary was initially buried in the old

Lutheran Burying Ground, but was later moved to Plot 306 of the Lewisburg Cemetery in 1848 or 49.[88]

Cameron, James, Colonel
1801-July 21, 1861

Born in Lancaster County in 1801, he studied law before getting involved with the Northern Central Railroad. He owned a farm near Milton, but listed Lewisburg as his residence. He also was a lawyer and served as superintendent of the Philadelphia and Columbia Railroad. He was brother of Simon Cameron, Lincoln's Secretary of War at the start of the Civil War. Simon nominated his brother for the position of Colonel of the 79th New York Regiment, a unit that wore kilts to reflect their Scottish heritage. Cameron was killed at the battle of First Manassas (Bull Run), the first Union Colonel and the first Pennsylvanian to die in the war. His body was initially buried on the battlefield, and it was not until a year later, when Union troops controlled the area, that it could be found. Local civilians helped identify the burial site. His body was recovered and put in a wagon for transport to Washington. Confederate cavalry captured the wagon, reburied the bodies in it, and took the wagon with them. Later in March, nearly a year after his death, Cameron's remains were again found and brought to Pennsylvania. Cameron was buried in Lewisburg and has an ornate tombstone with carvings of his hat, sword, and cape. His funeral was perhaps the most elaborate in the town's history.[89]

Cameron, William
October 15, 1795-September 10, 1877

Cameron was a tailor and riverman in his youth. He then served in the Northumberland Blues Regiment during the War of 1812. Cameron married Eleanor McLaughlin and raised his family in Lewisburg. He soon became involved with many important endeavors in the community. Cameron was involved with the construction of the Eastern Division of the Pennsylvania Canal, and directly oversaw the completion of the Cross Cut Canal that opened the trade to Lewisburg. Later he was a justice of the peace, ran a dry good store, and was involved with the Philadelphia and Columbia Railroad. He also helped established the Lewisburg Savings Institute (later the Lewisburg National Bank). In 1874 he donated $10,000 to the Borough of Lewisburg for a fire engine. Today the town's fire and rescue department is named in his honor.[90]

Chamberlin, William, Col.
September 25, 1736-August 21, 1817

Born in New Jersey, he fought at Monmouth, one of the largest battles of the Revolution. Governor Livingston of New Jersey sent him on important missions during the war, including purchasing supplies for the military. He settled in Union County in 1793 and became a prominent citizen. He served as a delegate, representing White Deer in the 1808 state Congressional Convention. Chamberlin had four wives: Elizabeth T. Broeh, Anna Park, Margaret Park, and lastly Mary Ann Kimble. With these four women, he was the father of twenty-three children.[91]

Dershem, Franklin Lewis
March 5, 1865-February 14, 1950

Born in New Columbia, Dershem attended Palm's National Business College in Philadelphia. From 1887-1891 he was postmaster of Kelly Point. He was also on the board of trustees for Albright College in Myerstown. Dershem served in the state House of Representatives in 1907, 1908, 1911, and 1912. He went to Congress in 1913, serving until 1915. Following a failed re-election, he served as auditor in the Philadelphia Division of the IRS from 1915 until his death.

Dull, Ralph J.
1899-September 26, 1918

As a private in the 103rd Trench Mortar Battalion, he was killed in September, 1918 in France, along with several other Lewisburg men. The town's American Legion post bears his name, along with that of fellow soldier Bright Kratzer.

Fetherston, Edith Kelly
1885-1972

Edith Fetherston was born in Lewisburg, and after traveling far and wide, returned to her hometown. She studied art in France, and married John F. Fetherston. She taught at art schools in Baltimore and Connecticut. Upon returning to Lewisburg, the Fetherstons bought the home at the corner of Water and Market Streets. Edith collected local decorative arts and furniture. She willed the house to become a museum, now known as Packwood House (named after the Fetherston ancestral home in England). Her personal collection of art became the basis of the museum's collection.[92]

Focht, Benjamin Kurtz
March 12, 1863- March 26, 1937

Benjamin Focht lived at 60 South 2nd Street. At age 18, he established the *Saturday News* in Lewisburg in 1881, serving as editor and publisher. Delegate to the Republican State convention in 1889, member of state House of Representatives from 1893-1897. Served in State Senate from 1901-1905. Elected to Congress in 1907, serving until 1913. After failing reelection he returned to the newspaper. While in Washington, Focht worked tirelessly to promote his plan for pensions, and became known as the "Father of Old Age Pensions."[93]

Frick, William
November 3, 1817-February 20, 1895

William Frick was a prominent citizen who became involved in many enterprises in the years before the Civil War. He was a canal barge manager, President of the Lewisburg & Tyrone Railroad, and President of the Company to Manufacture Buckeye Reapers and Mowers.[94]

Green, Abbot, General
1784-March 20, 1851

Green was extremely active in local and regional affairs. He was the son of Joseph Green, a Revolutionary soldier and early settler in the valley. Green was a civil engineer who was involved with the Eastern Division of the Pennsylvania Canal, built in the 1830s. He was active in organizing the Presbyterian Church in Lewisburg and in development of the University at Lewisburg (forerunner of Bucknell University). He was elected as Major-General of the 8th militia Division in 1842. Green lived on Market Street. He died the same year s the University's first commencement. Living as he did at the close of the eighteenth century and on into the middle of the nineteenth, he witnessed great changes in his lifetime.[95]

Harris, John Howard.
1847-1925

Harris served in the Civil War, attended the University at Lewisburg (Bucknell). He was President of Bucknell from 1889-1919, was a professor of Philosophy, and served as a Trustee. He was also a Baptist minister, and founded the Keystone Academy at Factoryville. His daughter Mary Belle Harris attended the University as well.[96]

Harris Monument

Harris, Mary Belle
1874-1957

One of Bucknell's famous "Three Marys," she was the daughter of John Howard Harris. She attended Bucknell University in the

1890s and studied languages. She became the superintendent of the Women's Prison in Blackwell's Island, New York, and later was head of the Federal Penitentiary for Women at Alderson, West Virginia. She advocated humane care of prisoners, and was at the forefront of social reform for prisons.[97]

Himmelriech, William David
September 11, 1842-1897

Himmelreich was a successful businessman and active supporter of his church, First Presbyterian. He was involved with the boat building and lumber industries, as well as a nail work and furniture company, and gas, water, and coal industries. He became presdiednt of the Union Bank in 1895, and was active in bringing the telephone company to the area.

In 1891 Himmelreich donated 500 books for a library, and his will left $15,000 for books for the library. Union County's public library was named in his honor when it was housed next to the Fist Presbyterian Church on Market Street in Lewisburg.[98]

Kelly, John
February 1744- February 1832

Born in Lancaster, fought in the Revolution both in the Continental Army against the British and in local militia actions against Indians. Modern day Kelly Township is named for him. Kelly moved to the area in 1769, and rose to become a prominent militia officer. During the Revolution he served both with the Continental army fighting the British and in the militia defending the region from Indian attacks. He fought with Washington's army at Trenton and Princeton, and was also in many small engagements in modern-day Union County, on the frontier. After the war he served as a magistrate for the County (Northumberland at the time). Kelly was a giant, both in local politics and in person, standing over six feet tall. He was initially buried at the Presbyterian burial ground on Market Street, with a monument.

His remains and the marker were later moved to the Lewisburg Cemetery.[99]

Kelly Marker

Kelly Marker. Note the detail with a cannon carved into the upper portion.

Kratzer, Bright
May 15, 1899- September 26, 1918

Serving with the 103rd Trench Mortar Battalion in France during World War I, he and several other Lewisburg men were killed by a German shell. The town's American Legion post is named for him and Ralph Dull.

Linn, James Merrill
1833-1897

James Merrill Linn taught Latin and Greek at Franklin and Marshall College in Lancaster, then returned to Lewisburg and became a lawyer. He joined the army after President Lincoln's call for volunteers in the spring of 1861. After the war he served as a lawyer in Lewisburg, and also wrote history. His most famous work is History of the Susquehanna and Juniata Valley. His brother, John Blair Linn, wrote one of the most important histories of the area, Annals of Buffalo Valley, Pennsylvania, a crucial source for anyone researching the Lewisburg area.[100]

Loomis, Justin
August 24, 1810-June 22, 1898

A well-educated and visionary person, Loomis served as President of Bucknell University during the traumatic period of the Civil War. A member of the Baptist Church and graduate of Brown University, he became President of Bucknell in 1858, serving until 1879. After the battle of Gettysburg he and other University staff went to the battlefield to look for Lewisburg natives who were killed and wounded. He also guided the school through difficult financial times. His most lasting mark on the school is the current President's home, built during his tenure in 1866.[101]

Ludwig, William II
August 29, 1780-May 129, 1855

Ludwig was a physician and one of the founders of the University at Lewisburg, later Bucknell. He served as a university trustee and was part of a committee that selected the school's location.[102]

William Ludwig II Grave

Mathewson, Christopher, "Big Six"
August 12, 1880-October 7, 1925

One of five initial inducted into the Baseball Hall of Fame in 1936, Mathewson was born in Factoryville. He attended Bucknell, and excelled both at academics and athletics, playing football, basketball, and baseball. Here he met his future wife, Lewisburg native Jane Stoughton. Drafted by the New York Giants, he pitched for seventeen seasons. Many of his records still stand (fourth all time in wins, third in shutouts, fifth in Earned Run Average). He threw for three shutouts in 1905 World Series as the Giants beat the Philadelphia Athletics, still an unbroken record. After playing he later coached for the New York Giants and was president of the Boston Braves. During World War I he served in the Chemical Warfare Division, and at one point was exposed to poison gas. He died of tuberculosis in 1925, a result of his wartime experience. Bucknell University's Stadium is named in his honor, and in 2011 the gates were re-dedicated.[103]

McCormick, Harry Elwood "Moose"
February 28, 1881- July 9, 1962

Born in Philadelphia, he attended Bucknell University. Moose played outfield for five years with the New York Giants, Philadelphia Athletics, and Pittsburgh Pirates. He played in two World Series with the Giants, both of which they lost (in 1912 to the Boston Red Sox and in 1913 to Philadelphia). For a period, McCormick and Christy Mathewson were teammates with the Giants. McCormick was the first pinch hitter in professional baseball. He married Lewisburg native Dorothy Walls, granddaughter of Eli Slifer and a Bucknell Graduate. Harry coached the Bucknell baseball and basketball teams from 1922-25. He later served as Director of Housing for the University from 1947-58.[104]

McClure, Harold M.
August 8, 1859- March 1, 1919

After attending Bucknell University, he served as judge of the 1Seventh Judicial District from 1891-1911. He also played baseball with the Philadelphia Athletics.[105]

Meixell, Joseph
1807-February 19, 1867

Joseph Meixell resided at Housel's Run in Northumberland County and was one of the founders of Bucknell University. He also served as a trustee for the school.[106]

Miller, George Funston
September 5, 1809- October 21, 1885

Born in Chillisquaque Township, Taught school while studying law, attorney in 1833 in Lewisburg. He built the home at 43 South 2nd Street and later built and resided at 54 South 2nd Street. He served on the board of the Lewisburg Cemetery and as President of the Lewisburg and Mifflinburg Turnpike Company, which connected the two towns in 1825. George was also on the Board of Curators of the University at Lewisburg from 1846-1882. He later served in the U.S. House of Representatives from 1865-69. He returned to law and was also President of the Lewisburg, Centre, and Spruce Creek Railroad. Miller worked to promoted railroads in the area, and finally succeeded in getting a rail line to Lewisburg in 1869.[107]

Moore, James III
October 15, 1807-July 4, 1882

One of the founders of the University at Lewisburg (later Bucknell University), and served on its Board of Trustees. Moore served on the committee that selected the school's location. He also helped found the Lewisburg Baptist Church.[108]

Ramer, George Henry
March 27, 1927- September 12, 1951 (KIA)

Born in Meyersdale, Ramer moved to Lewisburg and graduated from high school here in 1944. He served in the navy from 1944-46. Following his military service, he taught at both Lewisburg Area High School and Bucknell University. He then re-entered the military with the outbreak of the Korean War.[109]

Ramer served as a Second Lieutenant in Third Platoon, Company I, Third Battalion, Seventh Marines, 1st Marine Division. He was awarded Medal of Honor for action in Korea on September 12, 1951. His citation notes:

For conspicuous gallantry and intrepidity at the risk of his life above and beyond the call of duty as Leader of the Third Platoon in Company I, Third Battalion, Seventh Marines, First Marine Division (Reinforced) in action against enemy aggressor forces in Korea on 12 September 1951. Ordered to attack and seize hostile positions atop a hill, vigorously defended by well entrenched enemy forces delivering massed small-arms, mortar and machine-gun fire, Second Lieutenant Ramer fearlessly led his men up the steep slopes and, although he and the majority of his unit were wounded during the ascent, boldly continued to spearhead the assault. With the terrain becoming more precipitous near the summit and the climb more perilous as the hostile forces added grenades to the devastating hail of fire, he staunchly carried the attack to the top, personally annihilated one enemy bunker with grenade and carbine fire and captured the objective with his remaining eight men. Unable to hold the position against an immediate, overwhelming hostile counterattack, he ordered his group to withdraw and single-handedly fought the enemy to furnish cover for his men and for the evacuation of three fatally wounded Marines. Severely wounded a second time, Second Lieutenant Ramer refused aid when his men returned to help him and, after ordering them to seek shelter, courageously manned his post until the hostile troops overran his position and he fell mortally wounded. His indomitable fighting spirit, inspiring leadership and unselfish concern for others in the face of death reflect the highest credit upon Second Lieutenant Ramer and the United States Naval Service. He gallantly gave his life for his country.

Ramer Hall, a combat conditioning facility on the campus of The Basic School at the Marine Base in Quantico, Virginia, is dedicated to his him

Slifer, Eli
1818- May 18, 1881

Born in Chester County, Slifer moved to Union County as a child. His first language was German, and he later learned English. He worked on canal boats in Lewisburg before entering politics. Slifer resided at 32 South 2nd Street before moving into his better known house outside of town in 1861. He was elected State Assemblyman, State Treasurer, and Secretary of the Commonwealth. While serving in the state House of Representatives he authorized the legislation that carved Snyder County out of Union County. During the Civil War he was an important administrator in the state's war effort, working closely with Governor Andrew Curtin. Slifer was a partner in several business including a boatyard and agricultural tool company. Upon his death the *Philadelphia Times* wrote he was "one of the unobtrusively great men of Pennsylvania."[110]

Spyker, Henry.
August 29, 1753-July 1, 1811

Spyker served in the Revolution while living in New Jersey. He was an adjutant and paymaster for his unit. He then moved to Pennsylvania, and was in the Berks County Assembly. Moving to Lewisburg in 1797, he was a Justice of the Peace. He built the first brick home in the town, still standing at the corner of Front and St. Catherine Street.[111]

Tucker, Andrew Gregg
October 4, 1844-July 5, 1863

Tucker would be the first Bucknell graduate to die of wounds in the Civil War. He enlisted in 1862 at age seventeen, a month after graduating. Promoted to Lieutenant of the 142nd Pennsylvania, he was mortally wounded on the first day of the battle of Gettysburg. He survived until July 5th, living long enough to learn of the Union victory there. Tucker's comrades buried him on the battlefield with a wooden headboard. Later his mother, Margery, pastor Steven H. Mirick, Professor George Bliss, and University President Justin Loomis went to care for Union County soldiers wounded in the fighting. They found the grave and took the remains back to Lewisburg. In 1867, Lewisburg's Grand Army of the Republic Post (Union veterans organization) would be named in honor of Tucker.[112]

Tucker Grave

Wolfe, Mary Moore
March 31, 1874- October 18, 1962

One of the "Three Marys" of Bucknell, Mary Moore Wolfe was a pioneer for women in the field of medicine. An 1896 graduate of Bucknell, she spoke several foreign languages and entered the field of psychiatry. After Bucknell, she attended the Pennsylvania Medical College, then studied medicine at the University of Michigan. She was in the Women's Division of the Norristown State Hospital for the Insane, and like her contemporary, Mary Belle Harris, she advocated humane treatment of the mentally ill.

In 1913 she became the first superintendent of the Pennsylvania Village for Feeble Minded Women at Laurelton. She was also active in the movement for women to gain the right to vote. She helped form the Women's Suffrage Party of Union County in 1914 in an unsuccessful effort to gain the vote for women. During World Wars I and II she supported the efforts of the Red Cross and YMCA to assist troops overseas. She was also on the board of the town's new medical facility- Evangelical Hospital. She was the aunt of Mary Ellen Wolfe.[113]

Wolfe, Mary Ellen
January 27, 1845- November 15, 1860

Like her aunt Mary Moore, Mary Ellen Wolfe was one of the first women to advance in the medical field. When entered the Pennsylvania Medical School in Philadelphia but did not finish. She died of Tuberculosis before finishing her medical degree. She is not to be confused with Bucknell's "Three Mary's": Mary Moore Wolfe, Mary Bartol, and Mary Harris.[114]

Wolfe, Samuel, General
1878- 1962

Wolfe served in three conflicts, the Spanish-American War, World War I, and World War II, an incredible fifty years of military service. He was also a member of the William Cameron Fire Department.

Other Prominent Burials
(When possible unit and/or branch of service are noted)[115]

Revolutionary War Burials[116]
Brady, John Captain, Co. D, 12th Pennsylvania
Chamberlin, John Colonel
Chamberlin, William Colonel, 2nd Regiment, Hunterdon County, New Jersey
Christ, Adam, Sergeant, Anderson's Company, State Regiment
Dale, Samuel
Derr, George, Northumberland County Militia
Kelly, John. Colonel, Northumberland County Militia
McClure, Roan
Nesbitt, Alexander
Nevius, Christian
Seitz, George
Spyker, Henry, Colonel, New Jersey
Strickland, Timothy
Sutherland, Thomas, Lt. Col., Northumberland County Militia
Weiser, Christopher
Wilson, Hugh
Wilson, Thomas+
Wilson, William

War of 1812 Burials[117]
Cameron, William
Derr, George
Green, Abbott, General
Housel, William H.
Howard, Thomas S.
Kelly, Andrew
Linn, David
McClure, Robert
Martin, John
Nevius, Ralph

Silsby, Uriah
Whittaker, John
Wilson, Samuel
Wilson, Thomas

Mexican War Burials[118]
Aiken, James
Brady, John L.
Jackson, McFadden

Civil War Burials[119]
Airey, William R, Orderly Sergeant, Co. F, 43rd United States Colored Troops
Airey, Barton, Co. F, 43rd United States Colored Troops
Balliet, Thomas, Co. I, 101st Pennsylvania
Bennett, William A. Hospital Steward, 14th United States
Blair, Wilbur, 45th Pennsylvania, 201st Pennsylvania
Brant, Henry, Co. I, 192nd Pennsylvania
Brewer, David C., 2nd Lieutenant, Co. H, 51st Pennsylvania
Brooks, John Co. F, 49th Pennsylvania
Bryant, Charles L., Co. M, 1st New Hampshire Cavalry
Cameron, James Colonel, 79th New York
Chamberlin, Thomas, Corporal, 150th Pennsylvania
Chappell, Zachary, Co. B, 5th Pennsylvania Reserves
Clapp, Theodore Eaton, AMDD
Clark, Annabella Vorse, Nurse, General Hospital #3, Nashville, TN
Cornelius, Jackson, Co. D, 52nd Pennsylvania
Cox, William J., Co. G, 41st Pennsylvania
Cox, William Franklin, Sergeant, Battery K, 2nd Pennsylvania Heavy Artillery
Dewire, Alexander, Co. F, 51st Pennsylvania
Derr, John H. Co. G, 4th Pennsylvania
Dickey, Lester P. Co. I, 202nd Pennsylvania
Dodge, Edward R., Surgeon, Navy
Donachy, John, Co. A, 195th Pennsylvania
Donachy, William L., Co. E, 142nd Pennsylvania

Dull, Joseph S., Co. I, 202nd Pennsylvania
Eccleston, Charles, First Lieutenant, Battery L, Third Pennsylvania Heavy Artillery
Eisley, Phillip, Co. E, 131st Pennsylvania
Evans, Charles R., MD, Captain, Co. E, 142nd Pennsylvania
Flack, William, Co. C, 11th Pennsylvania
Graham, Henry Spyker, Sergeant, Co. F, 2nd Pennsylvania Cavalry
Grier, Thomas, 51st Pennsylvania
Gussler, John A. Co., C, 161st New York
Hann, David, Co. I, 202nd Pennsylvania
Harrison, Francis C, Maryland
Holtzer, Joseph, Co. H, 188th Ohio
Hutchinson, Andrew, Co. H, 56th Pennsylvania
Ireland, John W. 5th Pennsylvania Cavalry
Jordan, John M., Co. I, 5th Virginia
Kaler, John, Co. D, 150th Pennsylvania
Kennedy, William M. Co. E, 208th Pennsylvania
Kirch, Frederick, Co. D, 52nd Pennsylvania
Kline, Reuben, Co. E, 51st Pennsylvania
Knox, John H., Captain Co. D, 11th Pennsylvania
Kohler, David, Co. E, 53rd Pennsylvania
Lenhart, Henry Co. D, 52nd Pennsylvania
Lenhart, Benjamin, Co. I, 202nd Pennsylvania
Marsh, Charles K., Co. E, 53rd Pennsylvania
McBride, James Sergeant, Co. D, 52nd Pennsylvania
McCall, James, 144th New York
McFadden, Theodore H. First Lieutenant, Co. D, 5th Pennsylvania Reserves
McGregor, Charles, Musician, Co. D, 51st Pennsylvania
McPherson, John C., 4th Pennsylvania, 51st Pennsylvania
Milsom, John, Sergeant, Co. E, 53rd Pennsylvania
Murphy, Edward H. 5th New York
Owens, John A., Capt., Co. E, 142nd Pennsylvania
Penny, Charles A., Corporal, Co. D, 52nd Pennsylvania
Phillips, William L., Lieutenant, Co. D, 52nd Pennsylvania
Purcell, George, Co. H, 51st Pennsylvania
Reitmyer, David K., Co. I, 202nd Pennsylvania
Rock, William F., 8th Pennsylvania Cavalry
Rohrabach, James H., Co. H, 131st Pennsylvania
Shaffle, Joseph J., Co. H, 90th Pennsylvania

Shealor, Duncan K., Co. H, 156th Ohio
Schaffle, F.S. Co. E, 51st Pennsylvania
Smith, William C., Co. I, 12th Pennsylvania
Stapleton, George, Co. E, 142nd Pennsylvania
Sterner, Franklin, 51st Pennsylvania
Stoughton, Roalnd, Captain Co. D, 150th Pennsylvania
Thomas, John, Co. C, 188th Pennsylvania
Thompson, Brandy, Co. I, 8th Pennsylvania
Tucker, Andrew G., First Lieutenant Co. E, 142nd Pennsylvania
Tuttle, Charles E., Co. F, 7th Pennsylvania
Van Gezer, George Co. H, 51st Pennsylvania
Walls, Augustus G., MD, Surgeon, 20th Pennsylvania Cavalry
Waters, J.M., Co. I, 192nd Pennsylvania
Wertz, John H. Co. H, 4th Pennsylvania
Wetzel, Conrad, 28th Pennsylvania Militia
Wilkes, Newel, Co. A 5th Pennsylvania Reserves
Wilson, Francis
Woods, George D., Co. A, 11th Vermont
Young, Peter, Co. I, 192nd Pennsylvania
Yost, William, Co. B, 199th Pennsylvania
Zimmerman, William Co. E, 51st Pennsylvania
Zimmerman, William, Co. B, 8th Pennsylvania Cavalry

Spanish-American War Burials[120]
Ammon, Harry B. Cpl, Co. A, 12th Pennsylvania
Baker, Phillip P., Co. A, 12th Pennsylvania
Barber, William F., Lt. Col., Co. A, 12th Pennsylvania
Bower, Bryant Evans
Bucher, Abbott G.
Bennett, R. Morgan, Co. A, 12th Pennsylvania
Cornelius, Maurice L., Co. A, 12th Pennsylvania
DuBois, Charles A
Focht, Martin Luther, MD, Surgeon Major, Third Brigade, Pennsylvania Volunteers
Frick, George A.
Hafer, James, Co.D, 12th Pennsylvania
Hann, John F., Co. L, 21st Pennsylvania
Harris, Herbert F., Cpl, Co. G, 12th Pennsylvania
Hayes, Harold Lt., Navy

Lenhart, William Harrison
Marcey, Charles Henry
Peters, George, Co. F, 4th Pennsylvania
Pierce, Elmer, Co. A, 12th Pennsylvania
Poeth, John, Co. A, 12th Pennsylvania
Price, George, Co. G, 24th United States
Rine, Harvey L
Sassaman, Harvey, Co. F, 12th Pennsylvania
Weidensaul, Charles W.
Wetzel, Edward F.
Winegargden, Robert, Co. A, 12th Pennsylvania
Wolfe, Samuel B.

World War I Burials
Albert, Luther
Armer, Joseph
Aumiller, Charles P.
Aurand, Hayes
Aurand, John
Aurand, William C.
Auten, John Thompson, MD
Baker, Dale S.
Barber, William Neil
Bateman, Amos Eton
Baumgartner, Harry C.
Benfer, William F.
Bliss, Henry H.
Bower, Frederick Russell
Bowersox, Charles I.
Breisch, Leigh, MD
Bridge, William E.
Brough, Ralph E.
Brown, Irwin H.
Brown, Thomas Shoemaker
Byers, William B.
Carvell, William, Cpl., Battery E, 310th Field Artillery, 79th Division
Catherman, Earl Martin
Catherman, John I.

Cawley, William A.
Cleaver, Thoburn C.
Cleaver, Charles T.
Cobbett, Louis, MD
Cook, Arthur Watson
Cooley, Paul B.
Copeland, Daymond W.
Cornelius, Harold M.
Cornelius, Paul M.
Craumer, Luther E.
Cromley, John M.
Crossgrove, David Raymond
Crumling, Paul
Crumling, Sterling
Dietrick, Daniel Newton
Dietrick, Samuel Merrill
Dewire, Dale F.
Dieffenderfer, Warren J.
Dull, Ralph J., 103rdTrench Mortar Battery
Dunkle, Ira S.
Dupere, Alfred
Dyer, Albert J.
Earp, Harold E.
Eckenroth, John G.
Edwards, Robert Y.
Eister, David I.
Eisley, William C.
Eisley, Harold S.
Everetts, Arthur Andrew
Falls, John R.
Farley, Abram W.
Farley, Elmer L.
Farley, Walter Dayton
Feese, Orvis S.
Fees, Leroy David
Fischer, Anton
Garrard, Harold F.
Gearhart, Marshall Ellsworth
Gearhart, Reno C.
Gerber, Leslie D.

Gemmell, James R.
Gerhart, Weber L.
Gill, Earl Amson
Graham, Ferdinand C.
Groover, Clair
Groover, Robert L.
Grove, William Sherman
Gundy, Charles, MD, Medical Corps
Gutelius, Joseph C.
Guyer, William C.
Hann, Horace
Harriman, Phillip L.
Harris, Louis H.
Heimbach, Charles C.
Heiter, Oliver A.
Helbert, Harold L.
Herr, Watler M.
Hiatt, Lyle J.
Hillyer, Clive
Hitchcock, Francis Bennett
Holderman, Jesse Thomas
Hollenbach, George S.
Holter, Henry Walter
Hulsizer, Robert Leon
Irland, George A.
Johnson, George
Johnson, Joseph C.
Johnson, Miller A.
Johnson, Phillip E.
Johnson, William T.
Kline, Charles L.
Kline, Raymond D.
Kline, John W.
Kline, Paul A., Co. D, 111th Infantry
Kling, John W.
Kohler, Baker
Kohler, George B.
Kohler, Kinzie
Kohler, Ralph
Kohler, Stanton Uby, Lieutenant, Sanitary Corps

Kooney, Clyde R.
Koser, Ralph Samuel
Kratzer, Bright L.
Kunkel, George M.
Kunkel, Stanford
Lawson, George Benedict
Lebard, Frank N.
Lehr, John H.
Leisser, William III, MD, 1st Lieutenant, Medical Corps
Libby, Lyman C.
Logan, Ralph
Ludwig, Ammon F.
McCormick, Harry, Capt., 16Seventh Infantry, 42nd Division
McCullouch, Mark
McDonald, Ralph L.
Mabus, Earnest P.
Martin, Lloyd Roscoe
Mathewson, Christopher, Captain, 28th Division, Chemical Service
McClure, James Focht, US Army
Miller, George Corbett
Miller, George Funston
Miller, Luther F.
Montgomery, Walter Dewey
Morgan, Thomas S.
Morrison, Robert E.
Moyer, Elmer C.
Musser, Malcom E.
Myers, John A.
Myers, Stoughton J.
Myers, William C.
Neal, Robert M.
Neese, Albert L.
Nesbit, Malcolm Montgomery
Norris, Harry B.
Nace, Ralph
Noll, Herman E., 1st Lieutenant
Owen, Archibald, A.
Painter, William Graydon
Painter, James H.
Pangburn, Edward W.

Pardoe, Homer W.
Pelegrini, Ralph
Pennock, Cabel
Person, Hayes
Pross, Earl A., 314th Infantry, 79th Division
Pursell, Harry H.
Pursley, Louis A.
Rearick, Clarence V.
Reed, George
Reed, John Maxwell
Reed, Warren S.
Reedy, Ray B.
Reichelderfer, William A.
Renninger, Miles A.
Remaly, Mervyn W., Sgt, 35th Mtr. Amb. Co., Seventh Division
Rice, John, MD, 2nd Lieutenant, Sanitary Corps
Richards, Ralph Wallace
Richart, Dale M.
Rimert, Robert D.
Ritter, Thomas D.
Rote, Walter A.
Robbins, Harry R.
Romig, Gundy J.
Rooke, Robert
Rosborough, Elizabeth Lusk Nesbit
Roush, Harley Milton
Schmidt, Carl J.
Schulyer, William H.
Sechler, Ralph, Meixell
Sechler, Thornton
Shaver, Donald N.
Shott, John H.
Shultz, William Richard
Siglin, Charles E.
Simons, Alvin L.
Slifer, Elis S., Jr.
Smith, Robert Bruce, SATC
Snyder, Daniel George
Snyder, Joseph Whitmer
Showers, Irwin

Spaid, Hobard R.
Spyker, Baker Fairchild, 2nd Lieutenant, Co. G, 4th Infantry, Third Division*
Squires, John Henry
Stahley, Elmer
Starook, Elmer James
Stettler, George Ira
Stillwagon, Benjamin B.
Strassner, Charles F.
Starub, Ray N.
Sulouff, James Arthur
Swasey, Guy H.
Swinehart, Charles H.
Thomas, Fred C.
Thornton, Harry Ruhl, 1st Lieutenant, Medical Corps
Valentine, Roy S.
Vonada, Earnest
Wagner, Forest B.
Wagner, John M.
Wagner, Max S.
Walgram, Charles O.
Walls, Slifer E., MD, 1st Lieutenant, Medical Corps
Walter, John
Walter, John F.
Walter, Merrill Roy
Walter, W. Leiser
Waltman, Roy S.
Walkens, William W.
Weaver, Harry B.
Weidensaul, Harry B.
Wenzel, Lee Weaver
Wenzle, Starret
Wilson, Robert F.
Wolfe, Samuel B.
Yost, Amandus E.
Yost, Grover C.
Yost, James A., Sgt, Co. F, 109th Regiment, 28th Division
Yocum, Floyd Jacob
Young, James F., Battery A, 108th Field Artillery, 28th Division
Young, Raymond L.

Zeiber, George R.
Zechman, Silas M.

World War II Burials
Ague, Charles W.
Ammon, Roy, Co. K, 16Seventh Infantry
Ammon, William C, Staff Sergeant, Air Force*
Arney, Donald B.
Asprey, Albert J.
Aurand, James C.
Auten, William S.
Bailey, Reno E. Jr.
Baker, David M.
Baker, Lee William, Marines
Ballentine, George Newton
Baney Robert Sheasley
Beaver, Douglas N.
Bechtel, George Hamilton
Beisel, John Morris
Bell, John A.
Benfer, Guy E.
Benfer, William G.
Berge, John F.
Berger, Paul D.
Betzer, William H., Sr.
Bigler, Clarence William
Bingaman, Frank
Bingaman, William Isaac
Birchard, Robert T.
Blum, Sylvester
Blume, Albert M. K.
Bolin, Carroll Eugene
Bolin, Margaret Mary
Boop, Clyde W.
Boop, Eugene L.
Bordner, John C.
Bottomstone, Charles Albert
Boudeman, Elwood L.
Bower, Charles A.

Bowersox, Charles Ira Jr.
Boyer, Bryce O.
Bridge, Harold K.
Bridge, Harry Clavin
Bridge, Lewis F.
Bridge, Luther Edward Sr.
Bromfield, Malcolm P.
Brouse, George M.
Brown, Charles L.
Brzeskiewicz, John J.
Brzeskiewicz, Thaddeus
Burgess, Bernard J.
Burns, Robert Q.
Byrne, Patrick J.
Campbell, Clyde
Campbell, Franklin Eugene
Candrick, Thomas Robert
Carter, Joseph A.
Catherman, Forest, Jr.
Catherman, Warren A.
Chappell, Leroy Delbert
Clever, Helen Elizabeth
Collins, Sidney R.
Comerer, Robert M.
Condon, Stephen D.
Cook, Harold E.
Cornelius, Robert L.
Cornelius, William B.
Coup, Lee Ray
Crabb, Donald Ira
Cramer, Leon D.
Crawford, Irvine M.
Crow, Paul E.
Crowley, Leonard W.
D'Angelo, John J., Captain, Marines
Dale, Paul
Dauel, Robert A.
Davis, William C.
Dearman, Benjamin H.
Degling, Ewin G, MD

Delcamp, Chrales L.
Dennis, Rober Earl
Denius, Cliar L.
Derr, Fred M.
Derr, John W.
Dewire, Raymond Robert
Doebler, Sherman
Donachy, Neal E.
Dubaskas, E. Louise
Duck, William Oscar,
Dye, Richard A.
Earhart, Herman Marlow
Eberhart, Kenneth T.
Eberhart, Theron Charles
Edwards, Melre M. Jr.
Eicher, James M.
Emig, Albert O.
Erb, Elmer
Feaster, Walter A.
Feese, Ralph E.
Rennell, Edward Glenn
Fenstermacher, William E.
Fertig, Myron Lester, Air Force
Fetter, William Royer
Fisher, George Howard
Fisher, Kramer Fetzer
Falvio, Anthony F.
Flick, Alber LAure
Forbes, Donald D.
Forry, Marlin W.
Foster, Wiliam R.
Frantz, Jackson Hoffa
Gardner, Charles
Gardner, Rober A.
Gemberling, Roy D.
Gerber, Margaret Mary
Getz, Fred K, Jr., 13 W 390 GR 571 50 D*
Gilbert, Earl A.
Grower, William E.
Gramly, Neil Elmer Jr.

Gravell, Robert W.
Trenoble, John William
Groover, Clair
Groover, Robert Leroy
Grove, Ellen Holleran
Grove, Owen S., 11th Armored Division
Hackenburg, Arthur W.
Hafer, Arthur J. Jr.
Hafer, Donald E.
Hafer, Frank James
Haines, Chester S.
Haines, Lloyd F.
Haines, William R.
Halvorson, Bernard H.
Harris, James O. Jr.
Hassenplug, Elmer Homer
Heckman, Robert L.
Hector, Waldon I.
Heim, William A.
Heimbach, Harvey K.
Hirsch, Ralph Norman
Hoadley, Maxwell Edward
Hoffman, Charles F.
Holtzapple, George Henry
Holtzman, W. Richard
Howard, William Hoffman
Hower, Harold R.
Hufnagle, Howard S.
Hummel, Clarence, W.
Hummel, Harry J, Army
Hummel, Robert M.
Humphreys, Albert E.
Hyman, Charles Groover
Irwin, Raymond K.
Jacobs, Clinton H.
James, Margaret Beslin
Jones, Charles Hershel
Jones, Donald B.
Judy, John L.
Kalp, Charles Wolf

Kantrowitz, Seymour Nathaniel
Kauffman, Merrill C.
Kaufman, William Richard
Keister, Harry Paul
Kemmer, Albert B.
Kleppinger, Donald P.
Kline, Raymond P., Battery C, 190th Field Artillery
Kribbs, Benton A.
Krumrine, Robert W.
Kroh, Raymond
La Belle, Jules
La Form, William C.
Laird, Robert Stevenson, Army
Lane, William L.
Lapore, Frank M.
Lebkicker, Robert E.
Lee, Lester E.
Leitzell, Forest E.
Lemmerman, Charles
Letteer, John L.
Lewis, Thomas G.
Liebhauser, Edwin B.
Lockwood, Alfred R.
Long, Ernest L.
Long, Kenneth Matthew
Lower, O. Roan
Lucas, Fred U.
Lucas, John Ellis
McCarty, Charles William
McCormick, Harry E.
McDowell, David L.
McManus, Henry Arthur
Machamer, Donald N.
Machamer, Harold C.
MacIntyre, Herbert E.
Marks, Clark W.
Mathewson, Christopher Jr. Colonel, Air Force
McClure, James Focht, Army
Maurer, John Robert
Maurer, Maurice Albert

Meckley, Glenn E.
Mertz, Charles T.
Metger, Donald C.
Miller, Sidney Lincoln Jr.
Moran, James William Jr.
Moravick, William L.
Moser, Robert Burns
Moyer, Benjamin R.
Mooyer, Robert Clinton
Mull, Jay Edward
Mull, Wilmer A.
Murphy, Franklin J.
Meusser, Malcolm E.
Myers, James S.
Myers, John A.
Neal, Robert M., 2nd Lieutenant, 42nd CAC
Nehwadowich, Michael
Nesbit, Carroll C.
Nogle, Clarence
Nogle, William F.
Nyce, William E.
Osman, John
Owens, Eugene
Pacholok, John
Pangburn, Edward W.
Peterson, Francis, A.
Pittenturf, Freeman C.
Platt, John C.
Poeth, William C.
Polak, Emil J.
Powers, Harvey M. Jr.
Pursell, Donald Ross
Pursell, George Richard
Pursell, Robert Hudson
Quinlan, Edward James Jr.
Raidabaugh, John, Sgt, Army
Ranck, Glenn H.
Rankc, John W.
Ranck, Lee S.
Reagan, William Francis

Reed, Charles Palmer
Reed, William F.
Riechard, Franklin C.
Reigel, Bruce F.
Reish, George E.
Reitz, John H.
Reitz, Robert L.
Renninger, Leonard W.
Rheam, Michael C.
Rhoads, Robert W.
Rice, William Floyd, Navy
Ricketts, George J.
Rimert, William C. Jr.
Ritter, Eugene A.
Ritter, Kinwood C.
Rose, Harry Vernon
Rothermel, Alvin C.
Rowe, John E.
Rowe, Robert L.
Royer, Dayton Raymond
Royer, Torrence C.
Rudy, Walter G.
Russell, Thomas E.
Rute, Orval Elwood
Sanders, James C.
Savidge, Willis W.
Schulyer, Harold H.
Shaffer, John F.
Sheasley, Carl W.
Shiffler, Neal Fred
Showalter, Paul M.
Showers, Lee R.
Shrader, Pern W.
Simpson, James R.
Sitarsky, John J.
Slaterback, Charles P.
Slodosko, Victor
Smith, Amos B.
Smith, Arthur C.
Smith, Grover K.

Smith, Homer R. Sr.
Smith, Robert M., *USS Eisele*, DE 34
Snyder, Clair Francis
Snyder, Ronald W.
Stahl, John H.
Stapleton, Warren B.
Steele, Andrew B.
Stephens, John W.
Stoner, Dwight D.
Swinehart, William E.
Taraglia, Vito A.
Thomas, Fred C. Sr.
Thomas, George Edward
Thomas, George William
Thomas, Helen Witmer
Troutman, Edward Clark
Turner, James Lloyd
Turst, William S.
Tyson, Arthur R.
Ulrich, James L.
Ungard, Paul Emerson
Yarnell, Raymond S.
Van Buskirk, Leo Van
Volen, Wilson N.
Wagner, Clarence Earl
Wagner, John Millard
Wagner, Kenneth Norman
Wagner, Richard M.
Wagner, Richard Musser
Wagner, Robert E.
Wagner, Theodore L.
Walker, George J.
Walter, Blaine Gillespie
Walter, Donald J.
Walters, Melvin G.
Warren, Kenneth L.
Watson, George
Weary, John Lester
Wenrick, William E.
Williams, Louis A.

Wilson, Frank James
Wise, Donald Irwin Sr.
Wise, Harold M.
Witowski, Edward Joseph
Wolfe, Dorothy M.
Wolfe, Kenneth Dale
Wolfe, Samuel B.
Yarger, Curvin Seymour
Yocum, Theodore Lake

Korean War Burials
Difenderfer, Kenneth
Ramer, George Henry, Sec.Lt., 7th Marines, 1st Marine Div.
Rice, William F., Sgt, US Army

Vietnam War Burials
Chalver, William John, Navy
Minard, Charles W, Army

Statesmen
Dershem, Franklin Lewis
Focht, Benjamin Kurtz
Miller, George Funston
Slifer, Eli

Athletes
Blair, Walter Allen
Mathewson, Christopher
McClure, Harold M.
McCormick, Harry Elwood

Prominent Bucknellians
Harris, John J
Loomis, Justin Rolph
Ludwig, William H. II

Meixell, Joseph
Moore, James III

Physicians & Scientists
Harris, Mary Belle
Wolfe, Mary Moore

Prominent Lewisburg Residents
Cameron, William
Fetherston, Edith
Frick, William
Himmelreich, William D
Linn, James Merrill

*Buried overseas
+Buried at Presbyterian Church

Facts & Figures

Established in 1848
20,000 Burials
38 Acres
Oldest burial: November 2, 1848

Upon opening, graves from the Presbyterian (English) and Lutheran (German) burying grounds were transferred to the city cemetery in 1848-53. Among the most prominent was that of Colonel James Kelly.

The most elaborate funeral in the cemetery's history was that of Col. James Cameron, the first Union officer killed in the Civil War (at First Manassas). He was buried here in March, 1862. Numerous state and federal dignitaries attended, along with a military honor guard.

All of the cemetery's War of 1812 and Mexican War burials were veterans who outlived those conflicts.

Two of the Civil War burials are men who died ironically as the war was ending. Zachary Taylor Chappell was a seventeen year old member of the 5th Pennsylvania Reserves who died April 6, 1865, just three days before General Robert E. Lee surrendered at Appomattox. Chappell was a prisoner at the Confederate Prison in Salisbury, North Carolina. William Kennedy of the 203rd Pennsylvania died April 15th at a field hospital in Virginia, from wounds received earlier that month.[121]

There are 25 soldiers in the veterans section with two Civil War mortars and a World War I plaque.

One Confederate soldier is buried in the soldier section.

Over 100 Victorian family memorials are in the cemetery.

The cast iron fencing along Seventh Street dates to the 1880s.

At Seventh and St. George Street stands the boundary oak, from Derr's original survey of the town.

The Daughters of the American Revolution placed a marker at the boundary oak in 1935.

The Columbarium holds urns with the remains of several families.[122]

The Cemetery Today

The Lewisburg Cemetery is one of the community's most valuable historic resources. Cemeteries are easy to overlook, we tend to only go there for funerals or to visit departed family and friends. A walk through a cemetery such as this is equal to a visit to a museum or historic house. Here a visitor can learn about the town's history, its settlers, notable citizens, and achievements.

Organizations like the Cemetery Association require assistance to maintain and interpret this cultural treasure. The Lewisburg Garden Club maintains a garden near the Chapel. It is hoped that readers will be moved to support the cemetery and these organizations.

Lewisburgcemetery.org
570-524-9246

Sources

<u>African Americans in Union County: Slave and Free</u>. Lewisburg, PA: Union County Historical Society, 2012.

Alcorn, Sam. <u>Lewisburg, PA Cemetery</u>. CD Rom. Lewisburg, PA: Union County Historical Society.

Anti Masonic Star, April 17, 1835.

Baber, Lucy H.M. <u>Behind the Old Brick Wall</u>. Richmond, VA: National Society of Colonial Dames of America, 1968.

Bartol, Martha A. <u>Lewisburg Cemetery Transcripts, 1919-1924</u>. Lewisburg, PA, 1924.

Baumgartner, Donald J. "Benjamin K. Focht: Defender of Rural Conservatism," *Union County Heritage*, Vol. VI, 1978, 15-25.

Beers, D.G., and Pomeroy Beers. <u>Atlas of Union County and Snyder County, Pennsylvania</u>. Philadelphia, 1868.

Bickhart, Brian. Email to author. January 21, 2011.

Burke, Tammy. "Packwood House a Must-See in Lewisburg," *Union County Today*, 2011, 16-38.

Burns, Ken. <u>Baseball</u>. Inning 2: Something Like a War. Produced by Ken Burns and Lynn Novick. 107 minutes. PBS Home Video, 1994. Videocassette.

Ibid. <u>Baseball</u>. Inning 3: The Faith of Fifty Million People. Produced by Ken Burns and Lynn Novick. 120 minutes. PBS Home Video, 1994. Videocassette.

<u>Celebrating Our Two Centuries: Christ Evangelical Lutheran Church</u>. Lewisburg, PA: 2002.

Centennial History of the Building of First Presbyterian Church. Lewisburg, PA, 1957.

Charter, By-Laws, Rules and Regulations and Historical Sketch with List of Members, Plan of Grounds, and Financial Statement of the Lewisburg Cemetery Association. Lewisburg, PA: Press of the Journal, 1898. On file at Union County Historical Society, Lewisburg, PA.

Cook, Betty L. Union County and the Civil War. Lewisburg, PA: 100th Anniversary & Parade Committee, 2001.

Daughters of the American Revolution Patriot Index. Vol. III, P-Z. Baltimore, MD: Gateway Press, 2003.

Day, Sherman. Excerpts From Historical Collections of the State of Pennsylvania. Philadelphia: George W. Gorton, 1843.

Deans, Thomas R. Union County Sesquicentennial. Focht Printing Company,

Diblin, Joe, "Remembering a Lewisburg Native Legend," *Daily Item*.

Ibid., "From baseball to battle," *Daily Item*, June 12, 2011.

Downie, Johen W. "In the Spirit of 1776," in Charles M. Snyder, Union County Pennsylvania: A Celebration of History. Lewisburg, PA: Union County Historical Society, 1976, 25-36.

Dunkerly, Robert M. Stones River National Cemetery: Cultural Landscape Report. Unpublished Paper. 1996.

Eberly, Philip K., "Christy "Matty" Mathewson," in Bucknell Now & Then. Dallas, TX: Taylor Printing Co., 1995, 109-112.

Franks, Robert S. The Fighting Bradys of the West Branch. Watsontown, PA: West Branch Heritage, 2006.

Garrard, Martha, and Lydia Wetzell and E.L. Junkin. William D. Himmelreich Memorial Library and First Presbyterian Church. Lewisburg, PA: Foch Printing Co., 1948.

Groover, Claire. As It Used To Be. Winfield, PA, 1979.

Kalp, Lois. Silhouettes: Women of Union County. Lewisburg, PA, 1985.

Ibid. A Town on the Susquehanna. Lewisburg, PA: Colonial Printing, 1940.

Ibid. "The Three Marys," in Bucknell Now & Then. Dallas, TX: Taylor Printing Co., 1995, 65-67.

Ibid. "Lewisburg: People and Events That Shaped its History," in Charles M Snyder, A Celebration of History, pp. 116-36.

Ibid. "Bucknell University," in Charles M Snyder, A Celebration of History, pp. 137-48.

Lantz, Mary B. History of Lewisburg.

Ibid. Union County, Pennsylvania. 1966.

Larkin, Jack. The Reshaping of Everyday Life. New York: HarperCollins, 1989.

Leister, Gary E. Colonel James Cameron and the Soldier's Monument, Cameron Park, Sunbury, Pennsylvania. Sunbury, PA: Northumberland County Historical Society, 1996.

Lewisburg Cemetery Association Notes. Undated Document in possession of the author.

Lewisburg Cemetery Columbium Plan. Undated Document in possession of the author.

Lewisburg: History of Nineteenth Century Lewisburg
    Architecture. NP, ND.

Lewisburg Chronicle, March 18, 1862

Lewisburg Chronicle, March 21, 1862

Lewisburg Chronicle, May 6, 1899

Lewisburg Chronicle, May 20, 1899

Lewisburg Chronicle, June 3, 1899

Lewisburg Chronicle, July 15, 1899

Lewisburg Chronicle, July 22, 1899

Lewisburg Chronicle, December 16, 1899

Lewisburg Journal, October 24, 1913.

Lewisburg Journal, May 27, 1948

Lewisburg Journal, June 17, 1948

Lewisburg Journal, July 8, 1948

Lewisburg Journal, August 26, 1948

Linn, John Blair. Annals of Buffalo Valley, Pennsylvania.
    Harrisburg, PA: Lane S. Hart, 1877.

Marion, John F. Famous and Curious Cemeteries. New York:
    Crown Publishing, 1977.

Massey, Mary W. Early History of Lewisburg. Parts I & II.
    Unpublished paper, 1935

Mauser, I.H. Centennial History of Lewisburg. Lewisburg, PA,
    1885.

Pangburn, Jim. "Confederate soldier in Lewisburg Cemetery," *The Daily Item*, April 12, 2011

Parks, Gary W., ed. Ecclesiastical Architecture and Decorative Arts of the Susquehanna River Valley. Lewisburg, PA: Slifer House Museum, 2009.

Potter, Elisabeth and Boland, Beth. National Register Bulletin 41: Guidelines for Evaluating and Registering Cemeteries and Burial Places. Washington, DC: National Park Service, 1992.

Revolutionary War Soldiers of Union County, PA. Unpublished Paper. Union County Historical Society, Lewisburg, PA.

Rosenzweig, Roy and Elizabeth Blackmar. The Park and the People. New York: Henry Holt, 1992.

Schlereth, Thomas. Victorian America. New York: HarperCollins, 1991.

Sloane, David Charles. The Last Great Necessity. Baltimore: Johns Hopkins University Press, 1991.

Charles M. Snyder, "Transitions in Travel and Transportation," in Charles M. Snyder, Union County Pennsylvania: A Celebration of History. Lewisburg, PA: Union County Historical Society, 1976, 51-68.

Ibid. "Local Governance and Politics Across Two Centuries," in Charles M. Snyder, Union County Pennsylvania: A Celebration of History, Lewisburg, PA: Union County Historical Society, 1976, 69-91.

Ibid. "New Berlin and Limestone Township," in Charles M. Snyder, Union County Pennsylvania: A Celebration of History, Lewisburg, PA: Union County Historical Society, 1976, 92-115.

Ibid. "Union, East Buffalo, Buffalo, and West Buffalo Townships," in Charles M. Snyder, Union County, Pennsylvania: A Celebration of History. Lewisburg, PA: Union County Historical Society, 1976, 186-206.

Ibid. "Women Through the Passing Generations," in Charles M. Snyder, Union County Pennsylvania: A Celebration of History. Lewisburg, PA: Union County Historical Society, 1976, 259-290.

Ibid. "Union County's Role in World War I," in Charles M. Snyder, Union County Pennsylvania: A Celebration of History. Lewisburg, PA: Union County Historical Society, 1976, 291-307.

Ibid. "Union County's Role in World War I," *Union County Heritage*, Vol. XI, 1988.

Strangstand, Lynette. A Graveyard Preservation Primer. New York: Rowman & Littlefield, 1995.

The Daily Item, May 25, 2010.

The West Branch Canal. Sunbury, PA: Northumberland County Historical Society, 1996.

Trussell, John B.B. The Pennsylvania Line. Harrisburg: Pennsylvania Historical and Museum Commission, 1993.

Union County Planning Commission. Union County Historic Preservation Plan. Lewisburg, PA, 1978.

Union County Times, May 13, 1848

Union County Times, January 4, 1849

Veterans: Revolutionary War. Unpublished Paper. Union County Historical Society, Lewisburg, PA.

Welcome to the Historic Easton Cemetery. Easton, PA.

Wintjen, Elaine, "Pioneer Psychiatrist Headed Unique Facility," *The Daily Item*, April 15, 2011.

Ibid., "Civil War Veterans Began Memorial Day," *The Daily Item*, May 23, 2011.

Zeller, John F., "Our Baptist Beginnings," in <u>Bucknell Now & Then</u>. Dallas, TX: Taylor Printing Co., 1995, 11-20.

www.explorepahistory.com/hmarker.php?markerid=342 Accessed December 30, 2009.

www.johnsr.sneddenltd.com/historical/kelly.html. Accessed December 30, 2009.

www.livingplaces.com/PA/Union_County/Lewisburg_Borough/Lewisburg_Historic_District.thml. Accessed February 15, 2010.

www.wcec-lfd.org/history/wm_cameron.html. Accessed January 18, 2011.

www.first-presby.org/index.php/about/history. Accessed January 19, 2011.

www.vintageviews.org/vv-tl/pages/cem_monuments.htm#top. Accessed January 22, 2011.

www.genealogy.about.com/cs/symbolism/p/hands.htm. Accessed January 27, 2011.

http://randolphcountyillinois.net./sub65.htm. Accessed January 27, 2011.

www.itd.nps.gov/cwss/soldiers/cfm. Accessed 7 May 2011.

www.lewisburgcemetery.org. Accessed 23 January, 2012.

Ramer Display, Lobby, Union County Courthouse, Union County,

PA

Sign at Gatehouse in Cemetery

Index

American Legion, 33, 39, 53, 59, 66
Baker, J Thompson, 10
Beaver, Thomas, 10
Bucknell University, vi, 2, 18, 26, 31, 32. 33, 35, 36, 40, 44, 47, 50, 51, 53, 55, 56, 57, 61, 62, 66, 67, 68, 69, 70, 72, 74, 93
Buffalo Crossroads, 11, 38, 105
Cameron, James, 6, 15, 16, 50, 58, 76, 95
Cameron, William, 17, 30, 47, 50, 58, 75, 94
Cemetery Association, 7, 9, 10, 11, 19, 20, 23, 24, 26, 40, 43, 97
Chamberlain, John, 10
Chamberlin, John, 7
Chamberlin, William, 7, 9
Chapel, 23, 24, 25, 26, 40, 43, 44, 97
Christ, Levi, 10
Civil War, vi, 1, 4, 5, 11, 13, 15, 18, 19, 20, 31, 33, 39, 40, 42, 47-53, 57, 58, 60, 61, 66, 71, 72, 76, 95
Clingan, Flavel, 10
Donachy, George, 9
Dull, Ralph, 33, 34, 39, 52, 53, 59, 66, 80
Fetherston, Edith, 53, 60, 94

Focht, Benjamin, 44, 45, 46, 60, 93
Grand Army of the Republic, 11, 14, 20, 31, 40, 42, 50, 72, 105
Green, Abbott, 6, 7, 8, 49, 50, 61, 75
Gundy, Jacob, 10
Gundy, John, 10
Himmelreich, William, 44, 45, 63, 94
Hayes, Thomas, 10
Hayes, William, 10
Kelly, John, 6, 7, 47, 59, 63, 64, 65, 75, 95
Kratzer, Bright, 33, 39, 53, 59, 66, 82
Linn, James M, 19, 20, 47-49, 66
Linn, John B, 48, 66
Loomis, Justin, 18, 45, 47, 66, 72, 93
Ludwig, William H, 1
Lyndall, Stephen, 10
Mathewson, Christopher, 35, 36, 51, 55, 68, 82, 89, 93
Meixell, Joseph, 1
Memorial Day, 5, 18, 30, 31, 39, 40, 42
Mexican War, 5, 6, 42, 76, 95
Mifflinburg, 1, 6, 69
Miller, George, 10
Moore, James III, 1
Moore, James Jr., 10

mourning customs, 4, 5, 19
Nevius, Peter, 10
New Berlin, 1, 6, 7, 9
Noll, Henry, 10
Ramer, George, 54, 55, 70, 71, 93
Revolutionary War, 1, 3, 6, 11, 31, 38, 42, 43, 47, 49, 57, 59, 61, 63, 71, 75, 96
Ritter, Solomon, 10
Roland, George, 9
Ross, James, 10
Sheller, Hugh, 10
Spanish-American War, 39, 42, 74, 78
Sterner, Levi, 10
Tucker, Andrew, 13, 20, 31, 50, 72, 73, 78
Vietnam War, vi, 42, 93
War of 1812, 5, 18, 42, 58, 75, 95
Wilson, William, 10
Wolfe, Mary Ellen, 74
Wolfe, Mary Moore, 32, 37, 56, 74, 94
Wolfe, Samuel, 10, 74, 79, 84, 94
World War I, 33, 36, 38, 43, 53, 66, 68, 74, 79, 95, 106
World War II, 38, 53, 74, 85, 106

Notes

[1] Lois Kalp, A Town on the Susquehanna (Lewisburg, PA: Colonial Printing, 1940), 117, 119.
[2] www.livingplaces.com/PA/Union_County/Lewisburg_Borough/Lewisburg_Historic_District.thml. Accessed February 15, 2010.
[3] Lois Kalp, "Bucknell University," in Charles M Snyder, Union County Pennsylvania: A Celebration of History, 137. William Bucknell, living in Philadelphia, donated money for the school.
[4] Ibid., 58-9.
[5] Ken Burns, Baseball Inning 2: Something Like a War. Produced by Ken Burns and Lynn Novick (PBS Home Video, 1994) Videocassette; Ken Burns, Baseball. Inning 3: The Faith of Fifty Million People. Produced by Ken Burns and Lynn Novick (PBS Home Video, 1994) Videocassette.
[6] Lynette Strangstand, A Graveyard Preservation Primer (New York: Rowman & Littlefield, 1995), 1; Jack Larkin, The Reshaping of Everyday Life (New York: HarperCollins, 1989), 102-3.
[7] Thomas Schlereth, Victorian America (New York: HarperCollins, 1991), 292.
[8] John F. Marion, Famous and Curious Cemeteries (New York: Crown Publishing, 1977), 56; Schlereth, 292; Roy Rosenzweig and Elizabeth Blackmar, The Park and the People (New York: Henry Holt, 1992), 4-5; Elisabeth Potter and Beth Boland, National Register Bulletin 41: Guidelines for Evaluating and Registering Cemeteries and Burial Places (Washington, DC: National Park Service, 1992), 4-5.

[9]Marion, 56; Rosenzweig and Blackmar, 28, 107.
[10]Potter and Boland, 6; Schlereth, 292.
[11]Robert M. Dunkerly, Stones River National Cemetery: Cultural Landscape Report, Unpublished Paper. 1996, 9-10.
[12]Larkin, 100.
[13]Schlereth, 292; Larkin, 101.
[14]Schlereth, 292-3.
[15]Strangstand, 2.
[16]Ibid., 2, 5; Marion, 61, 64-7; David Charles Sloan, The Last Great Necessity (Baltimore: Johns Hopkins University Press, 1991), 77.
[17]Marion, 251. Many other communities claim to have started Memorial Day. In the former Confederate states an earlier date was chosen for Confederate Memorial Day.
[18]John Blair Linn, Annals of Buffalo Valley, Pennsylvania (Harrisburg, PA: Lane S. Hart, 1877), 502, 552; Lewisburg: History of Nineteenth Century Lewisburg Architecture, NP, ND.
[19]*Union County Times*, January 4, 1849; Mary B. Lantz, History of Lewisburg, 53.
[20]Linn, 556-7.
[21]I.H. Mauser, Centennial History of Lewisburg (Lewisburg, PA, 1885), 47, 54; Charles M. Snyder, "Transitions in Travel and Transportation," in Charles M. Snyder, Union County Pennsylvania: A Celebration of History, 56.
[22]*Anti Masonic Star*, April 17, 1835; Linn, 524.
[23]Revolutionary War Soldiers of Union County, PA. Unpublished Paper. Union County Historical Society, Lewisburg, PA.
[24]Charter, By-Laws, Rules and Regulations and Historical Sketch with List of Members, Plan of Grounds, and Financial Statement of the Lewisburg Cemetery Association. Lewisburg, PA: Press of the Journal, 1898. On file at Union County Historical Society, Lewisburg, PA, 5; Lucy H.M. Baber, Behind the Old Brick Wall (Richmond, VA: National Society of Colonial Dames of America, 1968), 9.
[25]Martha Garrard and Lydia Wetzell and E.L. Junkin, William D. Himmelreich Memorial Library and First Presbyterian Church (Lewisburg, PA: Foch Printing Co., 1948), 22; *Lewisburg Journal*, October 24, 1913; Gary W. Parks, ed. Ecclesiastical Architecture and Decorative Arts of the Susquehanna River Valley (Lewisburg, PA: Slifer House Museum, 2009), 53; Centennial History of the Building of First Presbyterian Church (Lewisburg, PA, 1957); *Union County Times*, January 4, 1849; *Union County Times*, May 13, 1848.
[26]Centennial History of the Building of First Presbyterian Church (Lewisburg, PA, 1957).
[27]Ibid.; Linn, 549.
[28]Linn, 321; Lantz, 50; Sherman Day, Excerpts From Historical Collections of the State of Pennsylvania (Philadelphia: George W. Gorton, 1843), 634.
[29]Welcome to the Historic Easton Cemetery (Easton, PA), 14.
[30]Ibid., 15.
[31]Kalp, 54; I.H. Mauser, Centennial History of Lewisburg. (Lewisburg, PA, 1885), 145; Charter, By-Laws, Rules and Regulations and Historical Sketch with

List of Members, Plan of Grounds, and Financial Statement of the Lewisburg Cemetery Association; 7.
[32] Linn, 512.
[33] Celebrating Our Two Centuries: Christ Evangelical Lutheran Church (Lewisburg, PA: 2002), 100.
[34] Snyder, 59.
[35] Mauser, 145.
[36] Charter, By-Laws, Rules and Regulations and Historical Sketch with List of Members, Plan of Grounds, and Financial Statement of the Lewisburg Cemetery Association, 6; Sam Alcorn, Lewisburg, PA Cemetery. CD Rom. (Lewisburg, PA: Union County Historical Society); Brian Bickhart, Email to author, January 21, 2011; Martha A. Bartol, Lewisburg Cemetery Transcripts, 1919-1924 (Lewisburg, PA, 1924), 1.
[37] Bartol, 1.
[38] Charter, By-Laws, Rules and Regulations and Historical Sketch with List of Members, Plan of Grounds, and Financial Statement of the Lewisburg Cemetery Association, 6.
[39] Ibid.
[40] Ibid., 7.
[41] Betty L. Cook, Union County and the Civil War (Lewisburg, PA: 100th Anniversary & Parade Committee, 2001), 26.
[42] Ibid., 40; Alcorn.
[43] Massey, Vol. II, 85; Jim Pangburn, "Confederate soldier in Lewisburg Cemetery," *The Daily Item*, April 12, 2011.
[44] *Lewisburg Chronicle*, March 18, 1862; *Lewisburg Chronicle*, March 21, 1862.
[45] Ibid.; Gary E. Leister, Colonel James Cameron and the Soldier's Monument, Cameron Park, Sunbury, Pennsylvania (Sunbury, PA: Northumberland County Historical Society, 1996), 5-662; Cook, 19-20.
[46] Ibid.
[47] Elaine Wintjen, "Civil War Veterans Began Memorial Day," *The Daily Item*, May 23, 2011.
[48] Ibid.
[49] Mauser, 145.
[50] Schlereth, 292-3.
[51] Ibid., 290-2; Larkin, 102.
[52] Charter, By-Laws, Rules and Regulations and Historical Sketch with List of Members, Plan of Grounds, and Financial Statement of the Lewisburg Cemetery Association, 7.
[53] www.livingplaces.com/PA/Union_County/Lewisburg_Borough/Lewisburg_Historic_District.thml; *Lewisburg Chronicle*, May 6, 1899; Lewisburg Cemetery Association Notes. Undated Document in possession of the author.
[54] *Lewisburg Chronicle*, May 6, 1899; Alcorn.
[55] *Lewisburg Chronicle*, July 22, 1899; Charter, By-Laws, Rules and Regulations and Historical Sketch with List of Members, Plan of Grounds, and Financial Statement of the Lewisburg Cemetery Association, 7.
[56] Ibid., 5; Sign at Gatehouse in Cemetery.
[57] www.vintageviews.org/vv-tl/pages/cem_monuments.htm#top. Accessed January 22, 2011.

[58] Ibid.
[59] *Lewisburg Chronicle*, July 15, 1899.
[60] *Lewisburg Chronicle*, May 20, 1899.
[61] Ibid.
[62] *Lewisburg Chronicle*, December 16, 1899.
[63] *Lewisburg Chronicle*, May 20, 1899; *Lewisburg Chronicle*, June 3, 1899.
[64] Lois Kalp, "The Three Marys," in Bucknell Now & Then. Dallas, TX: Taylor Printing Co., 1995, 66.
[65] Ibid.
[66] Ibid., 66-67.
[67] www.lewisburgcemetery.org; *Lewisburg Journal*, October 24, 1913.
[68] Burns, Vol. 2.
[69] African Americans in Union County: Slave and Free (Lewisburg, PA: Union County Historical Society, 2012), 37-39.
[70] Kalp, A Town on the Susquehanna, 159; John W. Downie, "In the Spirit of 1776," in Charles M. Snyder, Union County Pennsylvania: A Celebration of History, 31-32.
[71] Phillip K. Eberly, "Christy "Matty" Mathewson," in Bucknell Now & Then. Dallas, TX: Taylor Printing Co., 1995, 109-112.
[72] Ibid.; Burns, Vol. 3.
[73] Joe Diblin, "Remembering a Lewisburg Native Legend," *Daily Item*; Joe Diblin, "From baseball to battle," *Daily Item*, June 12, 2011.
[74] www.lewisburgcemetery.org.
[75] Bartol.
[76] www.lewisburgcemetery.org.
[77] *Lewisburg Journal*, May 27, 1948.
[78] *Lewisburg Journal*, June 17, 1948; *Lewisburg Journal*, July 8, 1948.
[79] Centennial History of the Building of First Presbyterian Church (Lewisburg, PA, 1957).
[80] Lewisburg Cemetery Columbium Plan. Undated Document in possession of the author.
[81] Alcorn.
[82] Ibid.
[83] Donald J. Baumgartner, "Benjamin K. Focht: Defender of Rural Conservatism," *Union County Heritage*, Vol. VI, 1978, 17.
[84] Mauser, 150; Bartol, 3. In 1919 the Cameron daughters were moved from Buffalo Crossroads.
[85] The National Park Service's online Civil War records website, the Civil War Soldiers and Sailors System, lists both men as with the 43rd USCT and having fought in Virginia. Further research failed to reconcile the discrepancy, thus I have relied on the information on their tombstones, assuming it to be the more accurate record of their service.
[86] George Ramer Display, Union County Courthouse.
[87] *Lewisburg Journal*, August 26, 1948
[88] Robert S. Franks, The Fighting Bradys of the West Branch (Watsontown, PA: West Branch Heritage, 2006), 39-40; John B. B. Trussell, The Pennsylvania Line (Harrisburg:
Pennsylvania Historical and Museum Commission, 1993), 134; Bartol, 1.

[89] Cook, 17; Leister, 1, 3-4.
[90] Kalp, A Town on the Susquehanna, 35; The West Branch Canal (Sunbury, PA: Northumberland County Historical Society, 1996), 59; www.wcec-lfd.org/history/wm_cameron.html.
[91] Kalp, A Town on the Susquehanna, 38; Lantz, 212; Revolutionary War Soldiers of Union County, PA. Unpublished Paper (Union County Historical Society, Lewisburg, PA), 6; Linn, 371, 440.
[92] Lantz, 212; Tammy Burke, "Packwood House a Must-See in Lewisburg," Union County Today, 2011, 16.
[93] Charles M. Snyder, "Local Governance and Politics Across Two Centuries," in Charles M. Snyder, Union County Pennsylvania: A Celebration of History, 87, www.livingplaces.com/PA/Union_County/Lewisburg_Borough/Lewisburg_Historic_District.thml. Accessed February 15, 2010.
[94] Snyder, "Transitions," 56, 122; Alcorn.
[95] Linn, 504, 539; Charles M. Snyder, "New Berlin and Limestone Township," in Charles M. Snyder, Union County Pennsylvania: A Celebration of History, 92-6, 108; Kalp, A Town on the Susquehanna, 33; The West Branch Canal, 59.
[96] Kalp, A Town on the Susquehanna, 165, 114; Kalp, "The Three Marys," 66; Alcorn.
[97] Kalp, "The Three Marys," 66.
[98] Kalp, A Town on the Susquehanna, 120.
[99] www.johnsr.sneddenltd.com/historical/kelly.html. Accessed December 30, 2009; Linn, 141-4, 153, 506; Charles M. Snyder, "Union, East Buffalo, Buffalo, and West Buffalo Townships," in Charles M. Snyder, Union County, Pennsylvania: A Celebration of History, 200; *Anti Masonic Star*, April 17, 1835; Linn, 505, 509.
[100] Kalp, A Town on the Susquehanna, 122
[101] Linn, 109, 263, 265; Cook, 24.
[102] Kalp, A Town on the Susquehanna, 119; Kalp, "Bucknell University," 138.
[103] Diblin, "Remembering a Lewisburg Native;" Phillip Eberly, "Christy "Matty" Mathewson," in Bucknell Now & Then. Dallas, TX: Taylor Printing Co., 1995, 109-112.
[104] Joe Diblin, "From baseball to battle," *Daily Item*, June 12, 2011.
[105] Kalp, A Town on the Susquehanna, 118.
[106] Ibid., 119; Kalp, "Bucknell," 137, 138.
[107] www.livingplaces.com/PA/Union_County/Lewisburg_Borough/Lewisburg_Historic_District.thml; Snyder, "Transitions," 59.
[108] Kalp, A Town on the Susquehanna, 57; John F. Zeller, "Our Baptist Beginnings," in Bucknell Now & Then. Dallas, TX: Taylor Printing Co., 1995, 12-13; Kalp, "Bucknell," 138.
[109] George Ramer Display, Union County Courthouse.
[110] www.livingplaces.com/PA/Union_County/Lewisburg_Borough/Lewisburg_Historic_District.thml.
[111] Linn, 294, 439; Daughters of the American Revolution Patriot Index, Vol. III, P-Z (Baltimore, MD: Gateway Press, 2003), 2541; Lewisburg: History of Nineteenth Century Lewisburg Architecture, 17.
[112] Cook, 23-4.

[113] Kalp, A Town on the Susquehanna, 130; Lois Kalp, Silhouettes: Women of Union County (Lewisburg, PA, 1985), 9; Charles M. Snyder, "Women Through the Passing Generations," in Charles M. Snyder, Union County Pennsylvania: A Celebration of History, 264, Charles M. Snyder, "Union County's Role in World War I," in Charles M. Snyder, Union County Pennsylvania: A Celebration of History, 295; Kalp, "The Three Marys," 66; Elaine Wintjen, "Pioneer Psychiatrist Headed Unique Facility," *The Daily Item*, April 15, 2011.

[114] Kalp, A Town on the Susquehanna, 131; Kalp, Silhouettes, 7-8; Snyder, "Women," 263.

[115] The lists of military veterans is as complete as possible, information was gathered by double checking sources with site visits.

[116] Massey, 89; Lantz, 203; *Lewisburg Chronicle*, December 16, 1899. During the Revolutionary War, Union County did not exist and the area was part of Northumberland County.

[117] Massey, 94.

[118] Ibid.

[119] Linn, 594-5.

[120] Massey, 90-3.

[121] Elaine Wintjen, "Civil War Veterans Began Memorial Day," *The Daily Item*, May 23, 2011.

[122] Bickhart.

www.ingramcontent.com/pod-product-compliance
Lightning Source LLC
Chambersburg PA
CBHW060409090426
42734CB00011B/2275